101 FACTS ABOUT DOLLY PARTON

The Unofficial Kid and Teen Quiz & Trivia Guide to the Country Music Star

Daisy Jolene

© Copyright 2024 - All rights reserved by Daisy Jolene

The content contained within this book may not be reproduced, duplicated, or transmitted without direct written permission from the author or the publisher. Under no circumstances will any blame or legal responsibility be held against the publisher or author for any damages, reparation, or monetary loss due to the information contained within this book, either directly or indirectly. You are responsible for your own choices, actions, and results.

Legal Notice: This book is copyright protected. This book is only for personal use. You cannot amend, distribute, sell, use, quote, or paraphrase any part, or the content within this book, without the consent of the author or publisher.

Disclaimer Notice: Please note the information contained within this document is for educational and entertainment purposes only. All effort has been made to present accurate, up-to-date, reliable, and complete information. No warranties of any kind are declared or implied. Readers acknowledge that the author is not engaging in the rendering of legal, financial, medical, or professional advice.

The content within this book has been derived from various sources. Please consult a licensed professional before attempting any techniques outlined in this book.

By reading this document, the reader agrees that under no circumstances is the author responsible for any losses, direct or indirect, which are incurred as a result of the use of the information contained within this document, including, but not limited to, errors, omissions, or inaccuracies.

THIS BOOK BELONGS TO:

Did you know?

Birth and Early Years

Imagine being one of twelve kids, singing and playing in the beautiful Smoky Mountains of Tennessee. That was Dolly Parton's life! Born on January 19, 1946, in Locust Ridge, she grew up surrounded by towering mountains and songs that filled the air. These sights and sounds helped Dolly dream big about music and stories, setting her on the path to becoming a country music star.

Family Life and Musical Influence

Even though Dolly's family didn't have much money, they were rich in music! Her mom's side of the family loved to sing and play instruments. In their cozy one-room cabin, music was more than just fun; it was a way for Dolly to express her feelings. Growing up in this musical atmosphere helped Dolly find her own amazing voice.

Did you know?

Early Performances

When Dolly was just a little girl, she started singing for people outside her family. She went on the radio and even TV, where her singing made everyone smile. By the time she was ten, she was on a show called "The Cas Walker Show," where lots of people got to hear her sing. This was just the beginning of Dolly's exciting adventure in music!

Songwriting Talent

Can you imagine writing a song at just seven years old? Dolly Parton did just that with her first song, "Little Tiny Tasseltop." Even as a little girl, Dolly had a special way with words, turning her thoughts and feelings into songs. This was just the beginning of her journey to becoming a famous songwriter who could touch people's hearts.

Did you know?

First Recording

When Dolly was 13, she recorded her very first song, "Puppy Love." She traveled to Louisiana to sing in a professional music studio. This was a big step from singing in her hometown to stepping into the big world of music making, where her voice could reach far and wide.

Move to Nashville

Right after finishing high school, Dolly packed up her dreams and moved to Nashville, a city where music floats in the air. Nashville was the place for a young singer eager to become a star. Dolly was determined to make her mark in country music, and this city gave her the chance to shine and share her music with more people than ever before.

Did you know?

Songwriting Breakthrough

In Nashville, Dolly began to shine not just as a singer but as a songwriter too. She wrote songs that other singers loved to sing. One of her songs, "Fuel to the Flame," became a big hit when sung by country star Skeeter Davis. This success helped Dolly make a name for herself in Nashville, proving she was great at singing and writing songs that captured everyone's heart.

"Dumb Blonde" and Rising Fame

Imagine stepping into the spotlight with a song called "Dumb Blonde." That's what Dolly did in 1967, and the song zoomed up the charts! But Dolly was quick to point out that the song's title didn't define her. She showed everyone she was smart and funny, turning a catchy tune into a chance to stand up for herself and make people laugh.

Did you know?

Partnership with Porter Wagoner

In the same year she made waves with "Dumb Blonde," Dolly joined a popular TV show hosted by Porter Wagoner. This was a big deal because it meant lots of people could see and hear her sing every week! Together, Dolly and Porter sang beautiful duets and made albums that many people loved. This partnership helped Dolly become even more famous and showed the world just how talented she was.

"Jolene" and Chart Success

Fast forward to 1974, when Dolly sang a song called "Jolene," which quickly became everyone's favorite and soared to the top of the charts. This song told a story that tugged at the heartstrings with its beautiful melody and touching words. "Jolene" showed just how good Dolly was at telling stories through her songs, making it one of her most famous tunes ever.

Show Off Your Dolly Smarts!

Which of the following awards has Taylor Swift NOT won?

    A) American Music Awards
    B) MTV Video Music Awards
    C) Billboard Music Awards
    D) The Nobel Prize in Literature

Which of the following awards has Taylor Swift NOT won?

    A) American Music Awards
    B) MTV Video Music Awards
    C) Billboard Music Awards
    D) The Nobel Prize in Literature

Answers

Which of the following awards has Taylor Swift NOT won?

A) American Music Awards
B) MTV Video Music Awards
C) Billboard Music Awards
D) The Nobel Prize in Literature

Which of the following awards has Taylor Swift NOT won?

A) American Music Awards
B) MTV Video Music Awards
C) Billboard Music Awards
D) The Nobel Prize in Literature

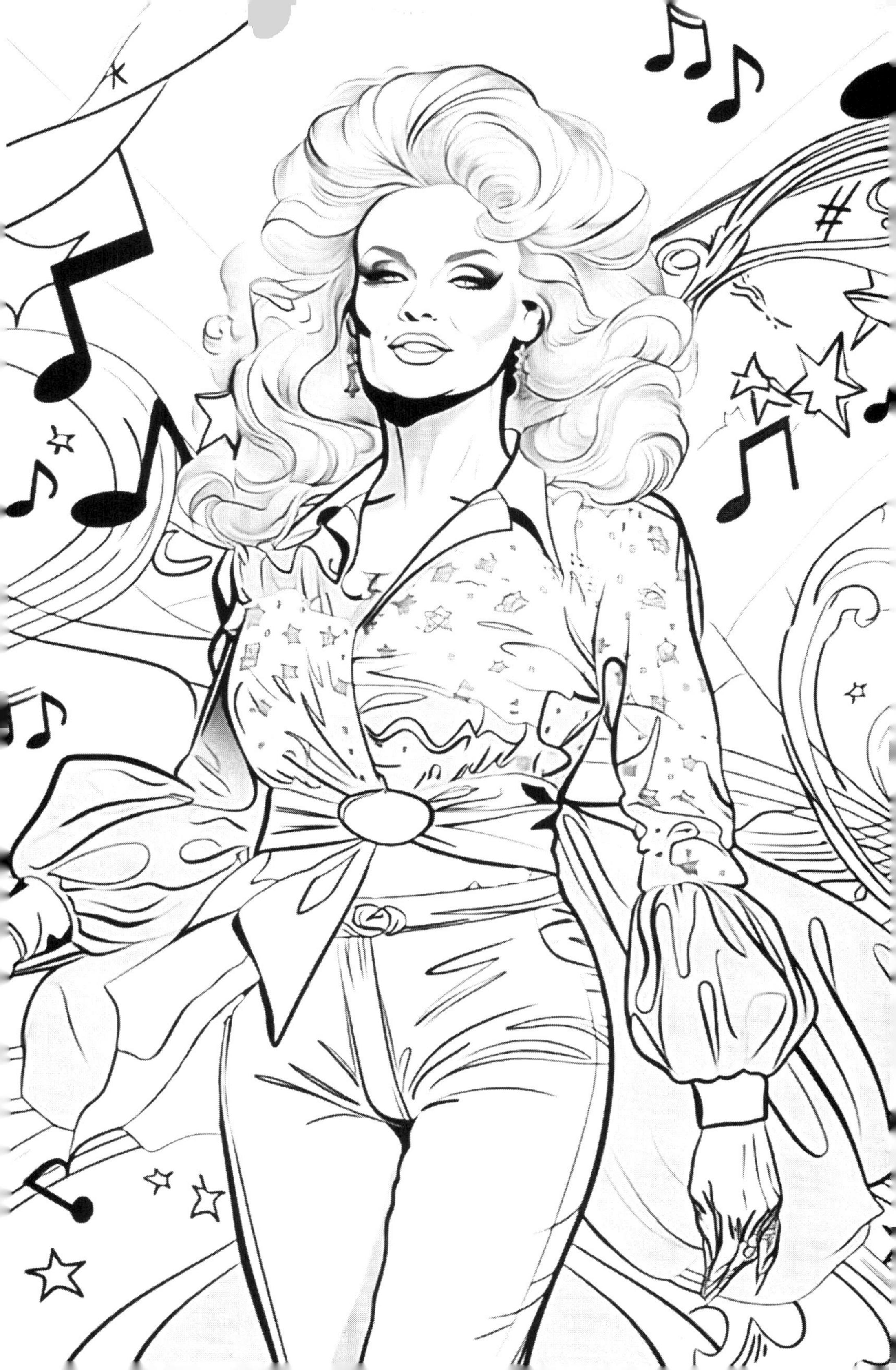

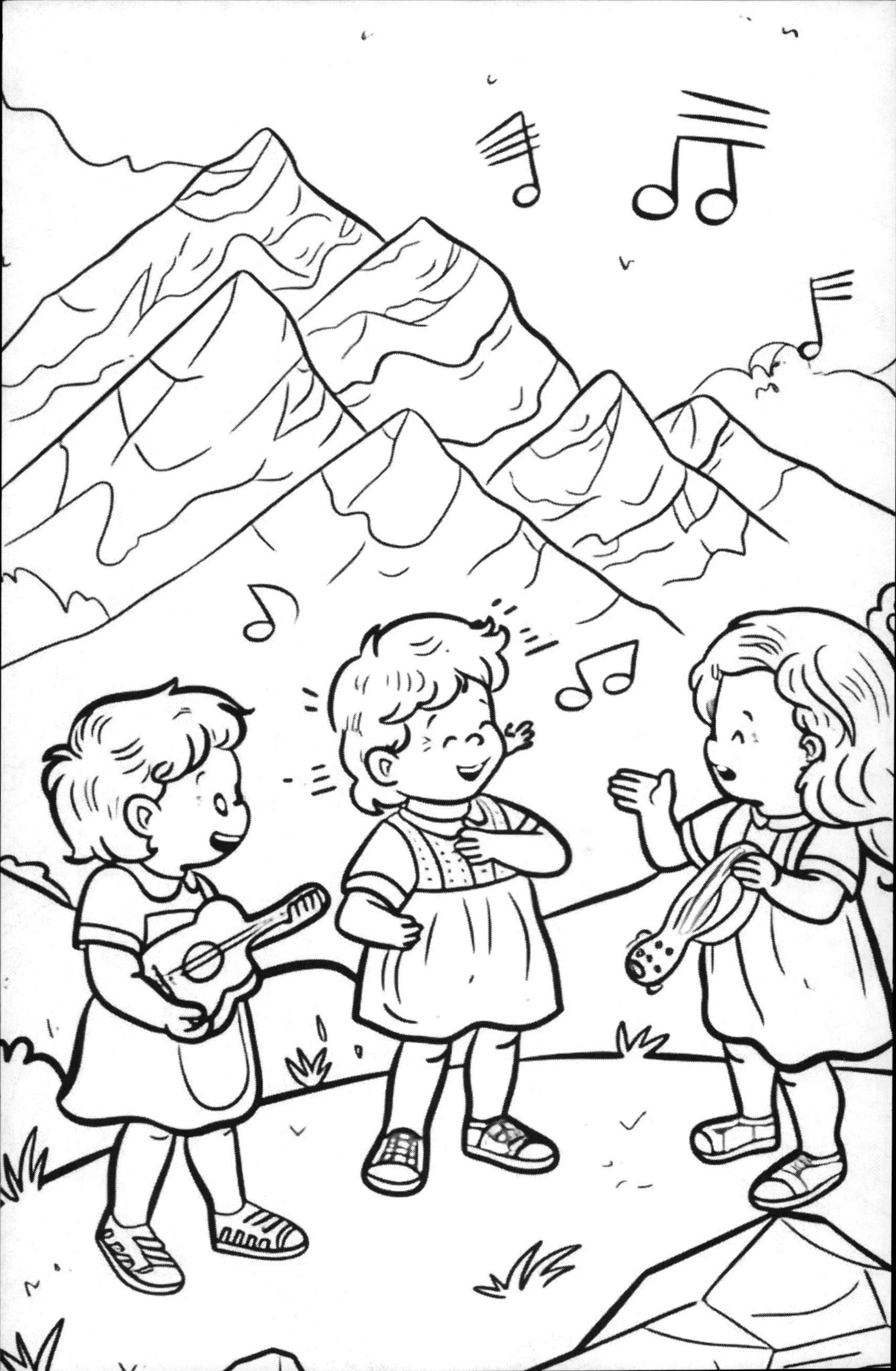

Did you know?

"My Tennessee Mountain Home" Album

In 1973, Dolly took everyone on a musical journey to her childhood with the album "My Tennessee Mountain Home." This album was like a scrapbook of her memories, filled with songs that shared stories about growing up in the simple, beautiful Smoky Mountains. The songs were like pages from her diary, giving everyone a peek into the places and moments that made Dolly the star she is today.

"I Will Always Love You"

Imagine having to say goodbye to a good friend. That's what Dolly did with her song "I Will Always Love You," written in 1973 to say farewell to her friend and music partner, Porter Wagoner. This song wasn't just a goodbye note; it became super famous worldwide, especially when Whitney Houston sang it in the movie "The Bodyguard." It's a song people still love to sing along to today!

Did you know?

Meeting the Queen of England

Dolly Parton has met many famous people, including the Queen of England! She was invited to perform at a special concert for the Queen and other members of the royal family, which was a huge honor and an unforgettable experience.

Inspirational Quotes

Dolly Parton is known for her wise and funny quotes. One of her most famous sayings is, "If you want the rainbow, you gotta put up with the rain." This quote teaches us that we have to go through tough times to enjoy the good ones.

Did you know?

Crossover to Pop Music

In 1977, Dolly tried something new by mixing country music with pop in her album "Here You Come Again." This wasn't just any album; it was a big hit that won her a Grammy Award! By blending these two styles, Dolly showed everyone she could sing any kind of music she wanted. This album made even more people love her songs.

"9 to 5" Movie and Song

Imagine writing a song that becomes the theme for a super funny movie! That's what happened in 1980 when Dolly wrote "9 to 5" for a movie of the same name where she starred with Jane Fonda and Lily Tomlin. This song is all about how hard women work and how strong they are, and it quickly became a favorite tune for lots of people.

Did you know?

Dollywood Theme Park

In 1986, Dolly created her own theme park called Dollywood in Pigeon Forge, Tennessee. Dollywood isn't just a place with fun rides and yummy food; it's a park where Dolly shares her love for the Smoky Mountains with everyone. By building Dollywood, she helped bring lots of visitors to her home state, helping the local people and showing off the crafts and music she grew up loving.

Imagination Library Foundation

Imagine a library that sends free books right to your mailbox! That's what Dolly started in 1995 with her Imagination Library. No matter where kids live or how much money their family has, they can get a brand-new book every month until they start school. It began in Dolly's hometown in Tennessee and now helps kids worldwide fall in love with reading. Isn't that magical?

Did you know?

Induction into the Country Music Hall of Fame

In 1999, the Country Music Hall of Fame welcomed Dolly Parton as one of its honored members. This was a big thank you to Dolly for all the wonderful songs she has given the world. It's like getting the gold medal in music, showing everyone that Dolly will always be one of the greatest country music stars ever!

Philanthropic Efforts

Dolly Parton loves to help people, especially in her home area in Tennessee. She started the Dolly Parton Health Foundation to ensure people can see doctors and get the medicine they need. Thanks to Dolly, lots of people are healthier and happier. She shows us that being famous is also about helping others.

Show Off Your Dolly Smarts!

1. What is the name of Dolly Parton's theme park located in Pigeon Forge, Tennessee?

    A) Dollywood
    B) Partonland
    C) Dollyworld
    D) Music Mountain

2. What famous song did Dolly Parton write to say goodbye to her music partner, Porter Wagoner?

    A) "Jolene"
    B) "9 to 5"
    C) "I Will Always Love You"
    D) "Coat of Many Colors"

Answers

1. What is the name of Dolly Parton's theme park located in Pigeon Forge, Tennessee?

	A) Dollywood
	B) Partonland
	C) Dollyworld
	D) Music Mountain

2. What famous song did Dolly Parton write to say goodbye to her music partner, Porter Wagoner?

	A) "Jolene"
	B) "9 to 5"
	C) "I Will Always Love You"
	D) "Coat of Many Colors"

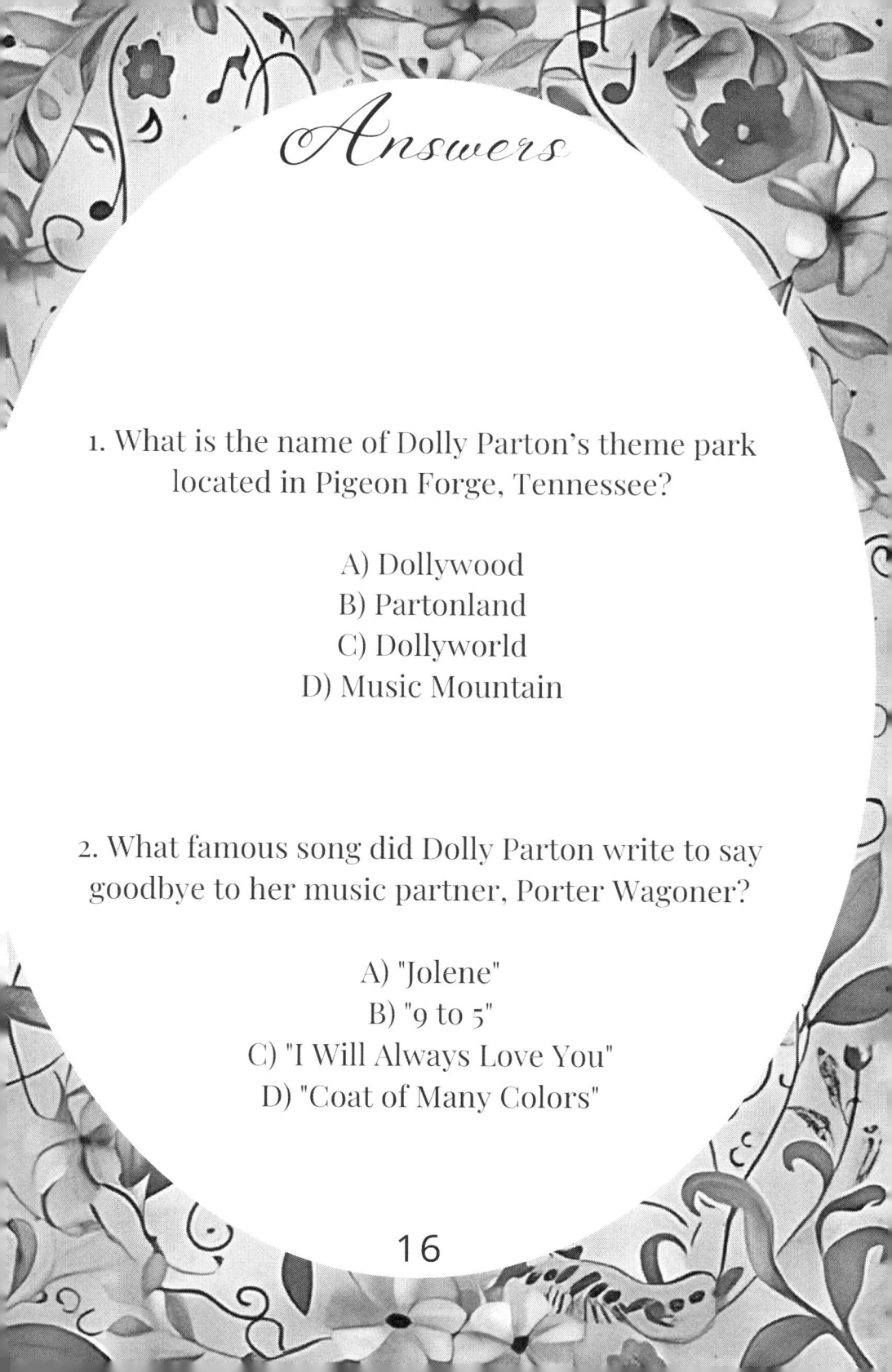

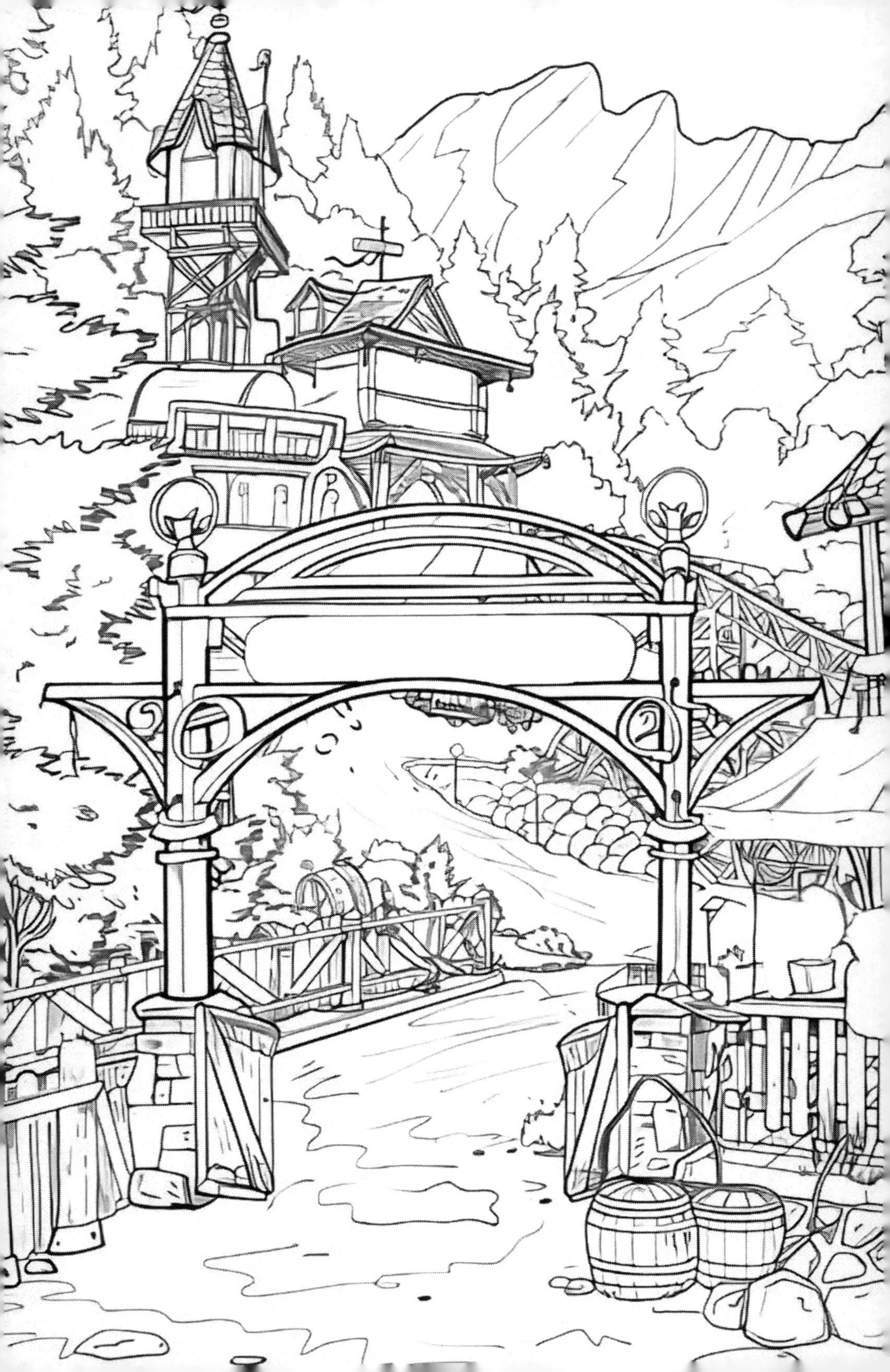

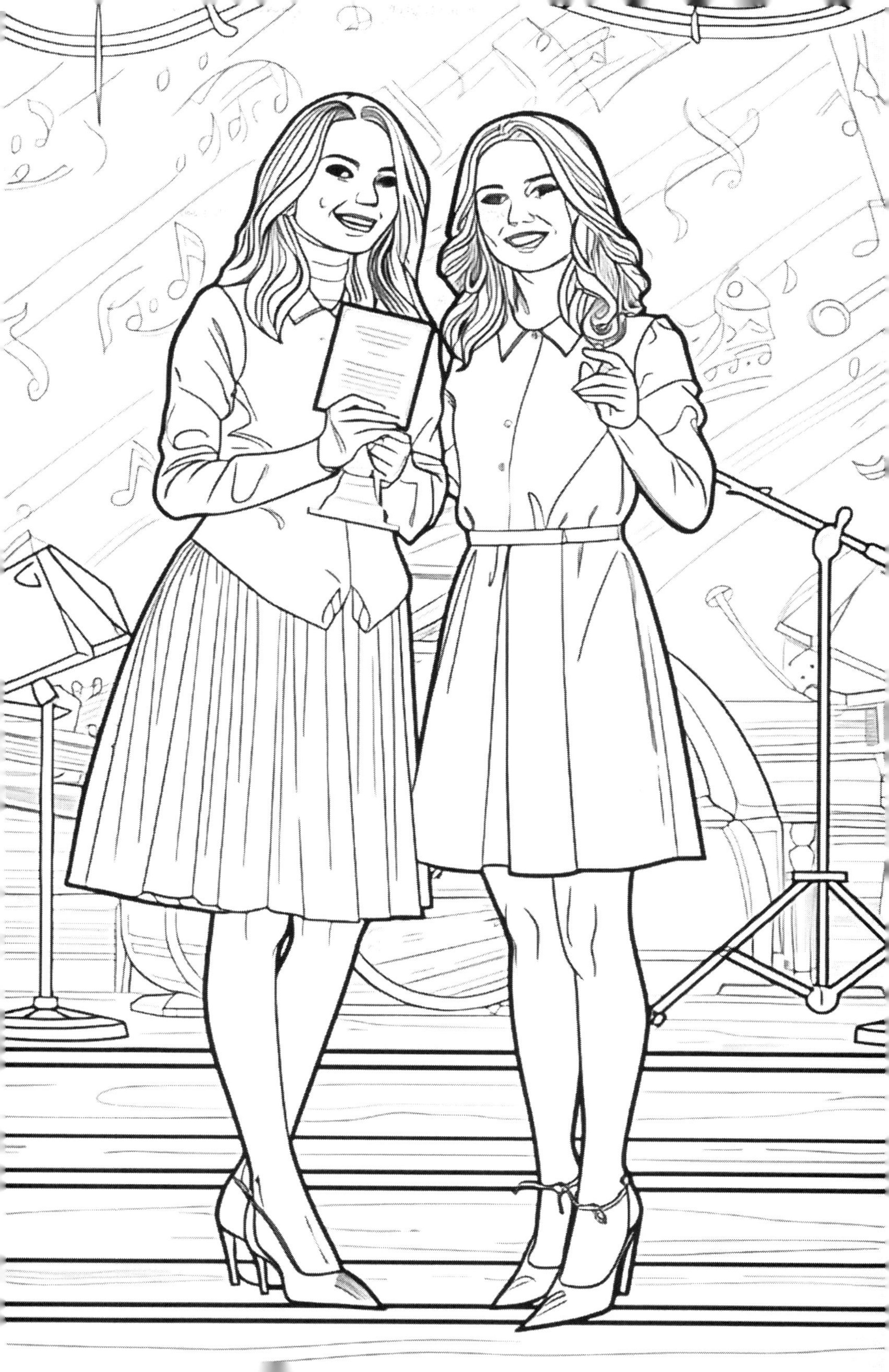

Did you know?

"Coat of Many Colors" Children's Book

In 2006, Dolly turned one of her most beloved songs, "Coat of Many Colors," into a beautiful book for kids. The story shares a sweet message about how being different is special and how we should be proud of who we are, no matter what we have. Dolly's book helps kids learn to be kind and accepting of each other.

Kennedy Center Honors

Dolly Parton was given a very special award in 2006 called the Kennedy Center Honors. This award is like a big thank you from the whole country, celebrating how much joy Dolly's music and movies have brought to people's lives. It shows that she's not just a singer or an actress, but a true star who makes America's culture richer.

Did you know?

Grammy Awards and Nominations

Guess what? Dolly Parton has been nominated for 50 Grammy Awards and has won 10 of them! That's like being picked as the best singer and songwriter many times over the years. This shows just how amazing she is, not just in country music but in all kinds of music. It's like she has a special trophy shelf just for her music superpowers!

Imagination Library's Global Impact

Imagine if you could give a book to every child in the world. Well, Dolly Parton's Imagination Library is almost doing that! Since 1995, this wonderful program has sent over 100 million books to kids everywhere, from Tennessee to faraway places across the seas. Every month, little kids get a new book to keep, helping them love reading and learning for their whole lives. Isn't that awesome?

Did you know?

Distinctive Fashion Style

Dolly Parton is not just a music star; she's also a fashion queen! She loves bright colors, glitter, and especially big, fabulous wigs. Each wig and outfit she wears tells a story, making her stand out as a true fashion icon. When you see someone dressed like Dolly, you just know it's going to be something fun and fancy!

Star on the Hollywood Walk of Fame

In 1984, something super special happened: Dolly Parton got her very own star on the Hollywood Walk of Fame! This star is on a sidewalk in Hollywood where only the most famous entertainers are honored. It's there because Dolly is amazing both as a singer and in movies. It's like a permanent "thank you" from the world for all the joy she brings to us through her art.

Did you know?

Marriage to Carl Dean

Dolly Parton met her husband, Carl Dean, on a sunny day in Nashville way back in 1966, right outside a laundromat—can you believe it? They've been married ever since, showing everyone what a true fairy tale looks like. Even with all the cameras and spotlight on Dolly, she and Carl have kept their life together sweet and simple, just like they like it.

Refusal to Retire

Imagine loving to sing and write songs so much that you never want to stop—that's exactly how Dolly feels about her music! She once said, "I'll be on my deathbed saying, 'One more song, one more song!'" This shows just how much she loves making music and how she never wants to give it up, no matter how old she gets.

Did you know?

Donation to COVID-19 Vaccine Research

In 2020, when the world was facing a big challenge, Dolly didn't just sit back; she helped out by donating $1 million to help find a vaccine for COVID-19. Thanks to her big heart, scientists were able to work faster on a vaccine that helps keep everyone safe from the virus. Isn't it wonderful how music stars can help save the world, too?

Godmother to Miley Cyrus

Did you know that Dolly Parton is Miley Cyrus's godmother? That's right! Dolly has always been there to offer advice and support to Miley, just like a fairy godmother in music. It's a special bond that shows how Dolly loves to help new singers shine bright, just like she has.

Show Off Your Dolly Smarts!

3. How many Grammy Awards has Dolly Parton won?

    A) 5
    B) 10
    C) 15
    D) 20

4. What is the name of Dolly Parton's literacy program that sends free books to children?

    A) Dolly's Book Club
    B) Reading with Dolly
    C) Dolly's Library
    D) Imagination Library

Answers

3. How many Grammy Awards has Dolly Parton won?

   A) 5
   B) 10
   C) 15
   D) 20

4. What is the name of Dolly Parton's literacy program that sends free books to children?

   A) Dolly's Book Club
   B) Reading with Dolly
   C) Dolly's Library
   D) Imagination Library

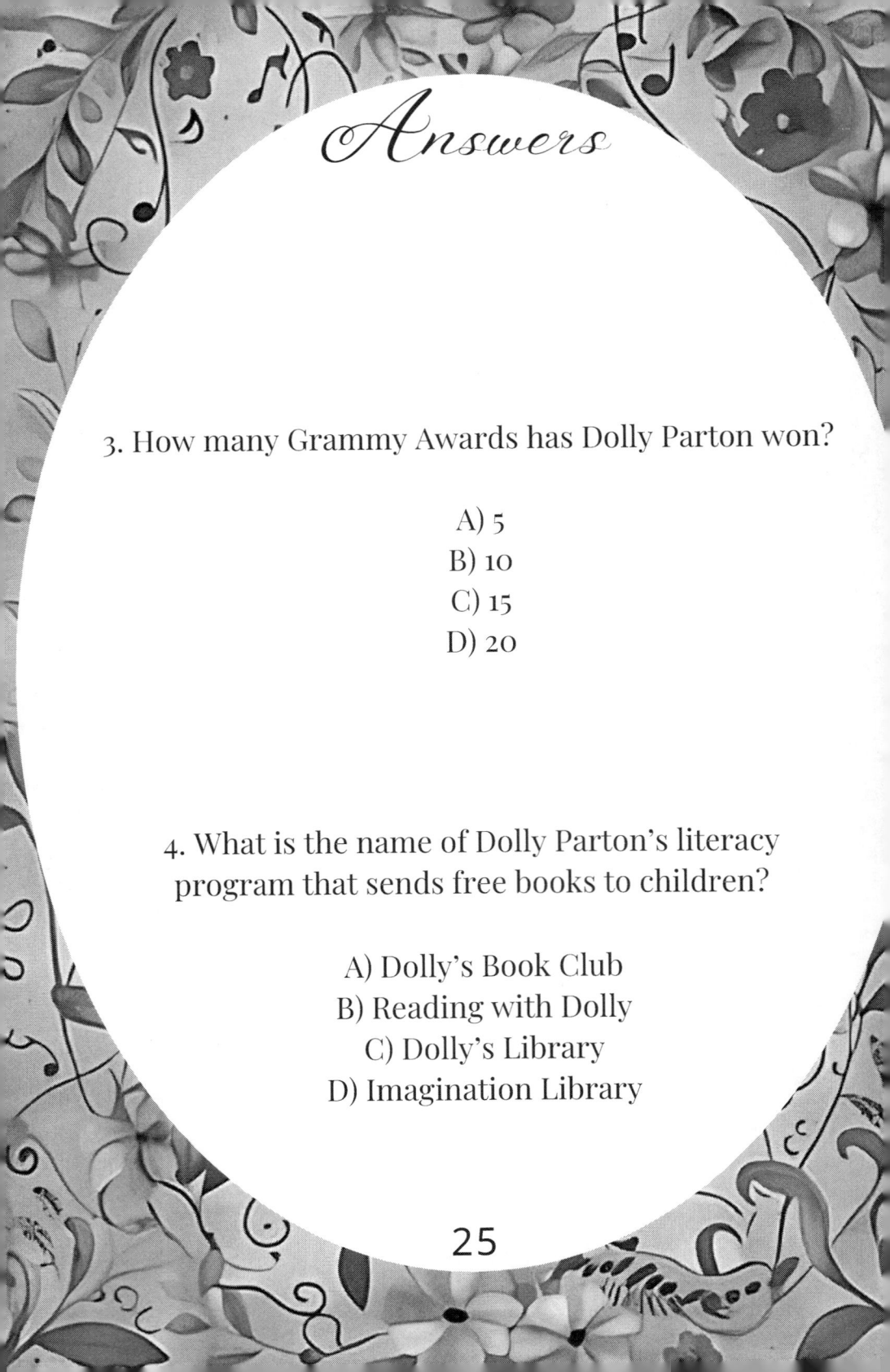

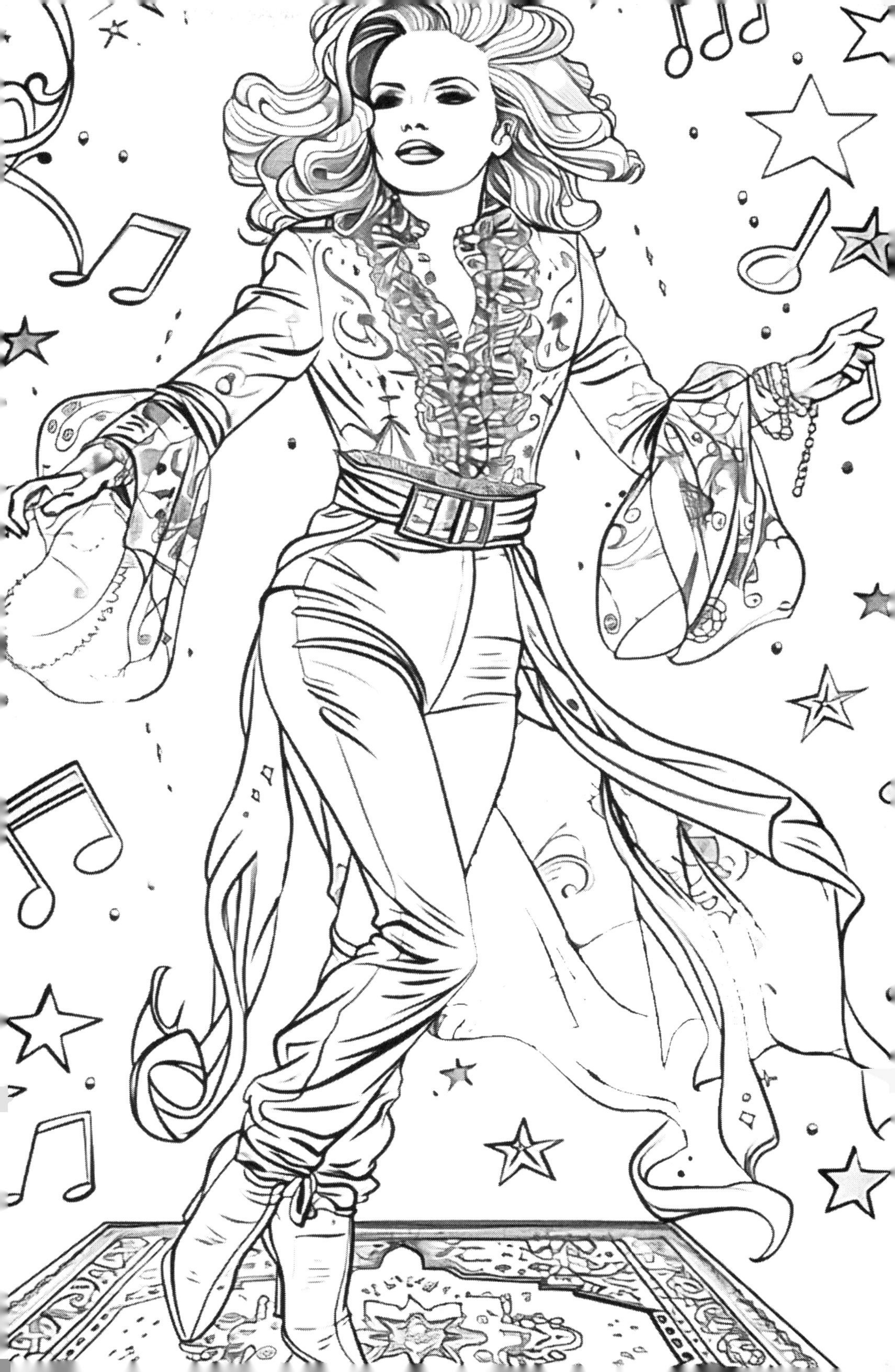

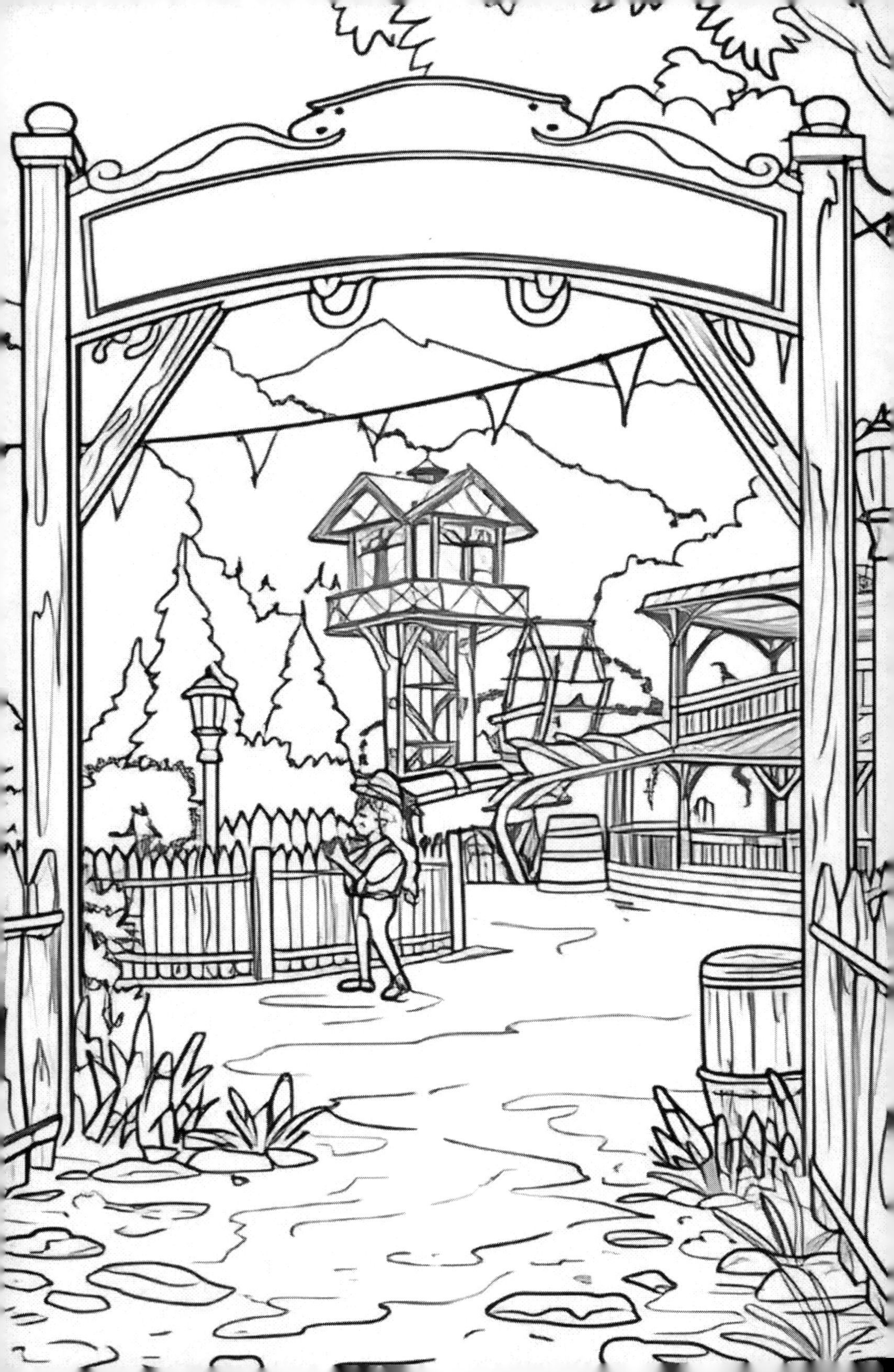

Did you know?

Favorite Food

Dolly's all-time favorite dish is chicken and dumplings, a yummy Southern specialty that reminds her of home in Tennessee. It's a warm, comforting meal that takes her back to her roots and family gatherings filled with laughter and love. Just thinking about it makes her smile, and probably makes her a bit hungry, too!

Refusal to Retire

Imagine loving to sing and write songs so much that you never want to stop—that's exactly how Dolly feels about her music! She once said, "I'll be on my deathbed saying, 'One more song, one more song!'" This shows just how much she loves making music and how she never wants to give it up, no matter how old she gets.

Did you know?

Private Life

Even though Dolly Parton is super famous, she likes to keep her personal life private. She doesn't talk much about her husband, Carl Dean, or other personal things when she's in the spotlight. This way, she enjoys her fame while having a peaceful, happy life at home, where it's quiet and calm.

Quick Wit and Humor

Did you know Dolly Parton is not just a great singer but also really funny? She loves making jokes, especially about herself, and that makes everyone like her even more! Her laughter and jokes show that she doesn't take everything too seriously, which is one of the reasons so many people love her.

Did you know?

Inspiration for Iconic Look

Guess where Dolly got the idea for her fancy style? From a lady in her town who was always dressed up! Dolly thought she was the most beautiful woman ever, and that's how she decided she wanted to sparkle and shine, too. It's a fun reminder that beauty can be found in unexpected places and people.

Family Involvement

Dolly Parton may not have kids of her own, but she's like a second mom to her nieces and nephews. She spends lots of time with them, showing how much she loves being part of her family. This love for family is something you can hear in her music, where she sings about the people and places that mean a lot to her.

Did you know?

Chapel for Reflection

Dolly has a special little chapel at her home in Tennessee where she goes to think and find peace. It's her quiet spot to sit and reflect, away from all the hustle and bustle of her busy life. This chapel is a peaceful place where Dolly can recharge her batteries and feel calm.

Honorary Degrees

Did you know that Dolly Parton is not just famous for her music but also super smart? Some really important schools, like the University of Tennessee and Harvard University, have given her special diplomas called honorary degrees. These are big thank-yous for all the wonderful music she's made, the help she's given to others, and for being an amazing example for people everywhere.

Did you know?

"Smoky Mountain Memories"

Imagine missing your beautiful mountain home so much that you write a song about it. That's what Dolly did with "Smoky Mountain Memories." This song is like a postcard from her heart, sending love to the hills and valleys of Tennessee where she grew up. It shows how much she loves her home and remembers the good old days of her childhood.

Songwriting Prowess

Dolly Parton has written over 3,000 songs! Can you believe it? That's like writing a new song every day for almost 10 years. Her songs talk about everything from her feelings and dreams to stories about people she knows. With every song, she shares a little piece of her heart, making her one of the best songwriters ever.

Show Off Your Dolly Smarts!

5. Which musical instrument does Dolly Parton famously use her acrylic nails as picks for?

A) Banjo
B) Guitar
C) Piano
D) Violin

6. What is the title of Dolly Parton's song inspired by a colorful coat her mother made for her?

A) "Rainbow Jacket"
B) "Coat of Many Colors"
C) "Patchwork Quilt"
D) "Mother's Gift"

Answers

5. Which musical instrument does Dolly Parton famously use her acrylic nails as picks for?

   A) Banjo
   B) Guitar
   C) Piano
   D) Violin

6. What is the title of Dolly Parton's song inspired by a colorful coat her mother made for her?

   A) "Rainbow Jacket"
   B) "Coat of Many Colors"
   C) "Patchwork Quilt"
   D) "Mother's Gift"

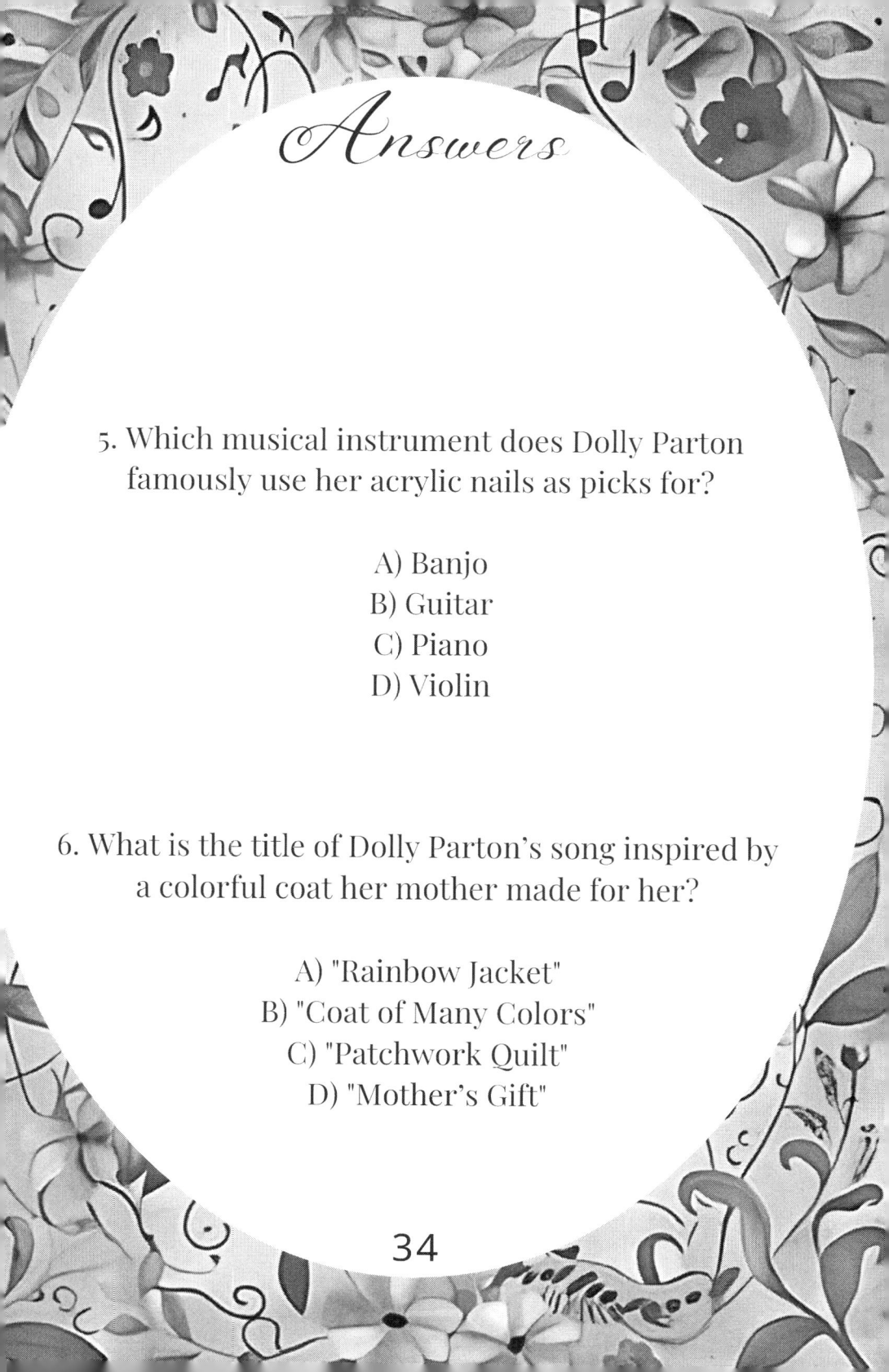

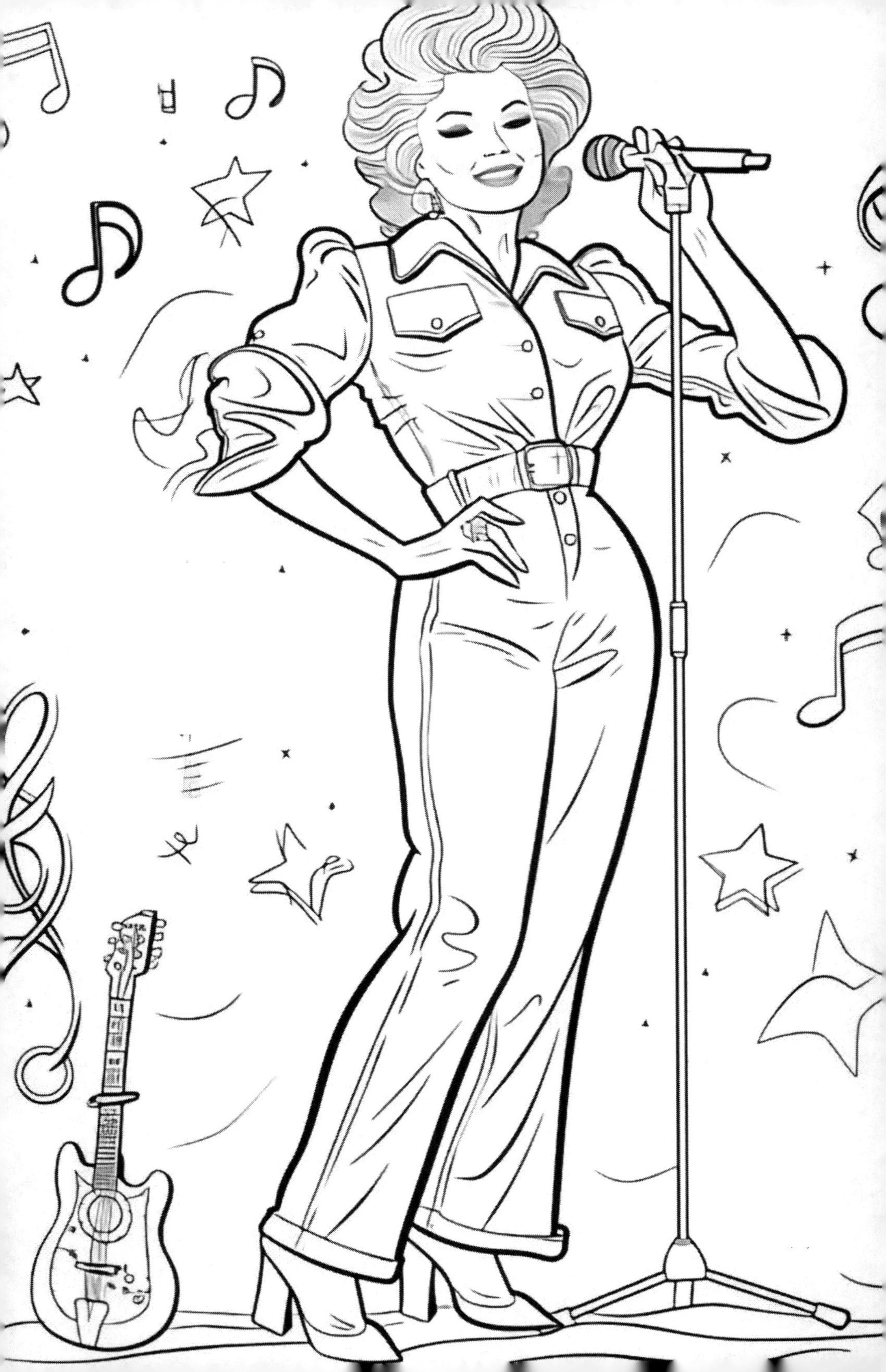

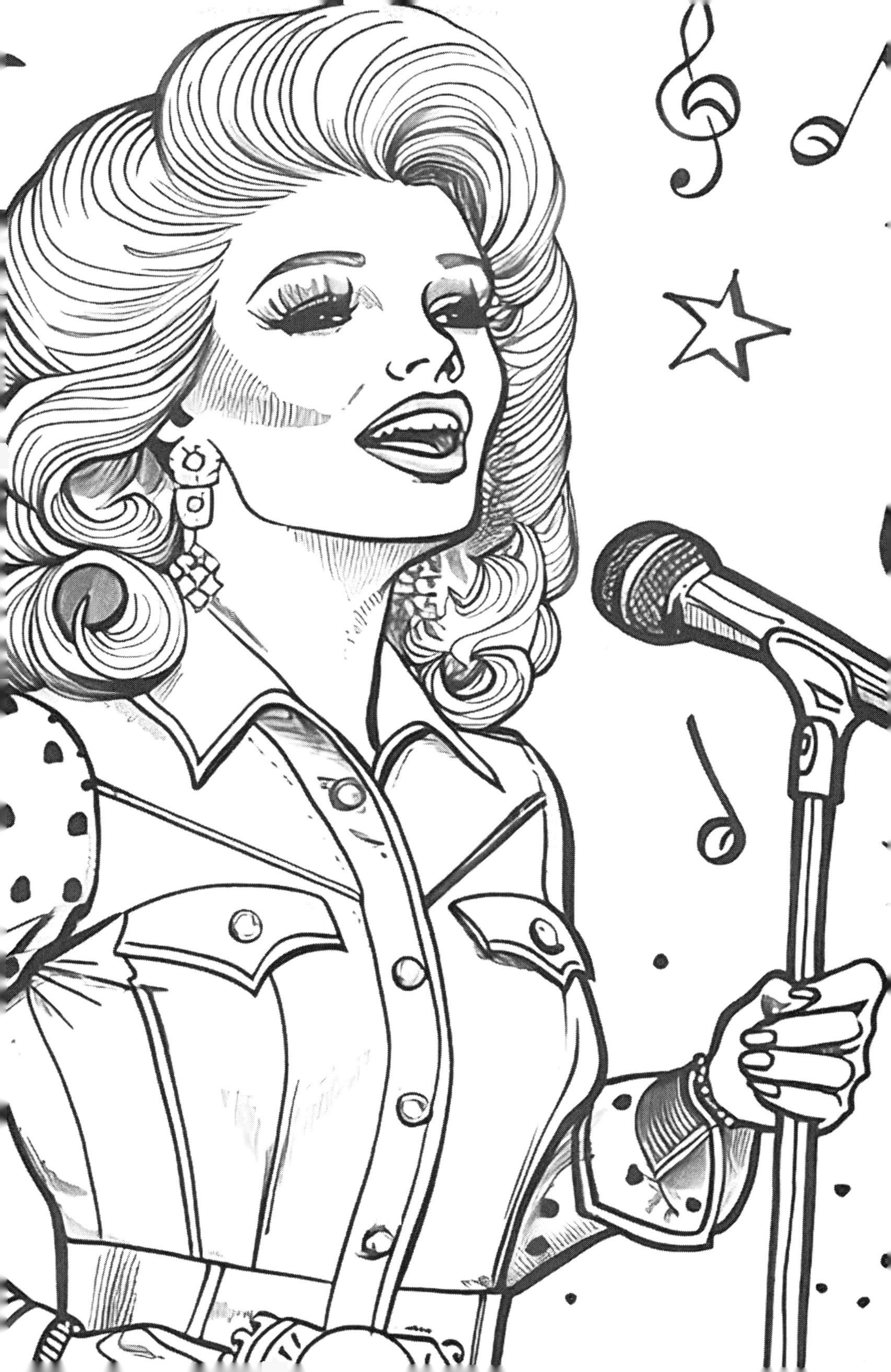

Did you know?

Look-alike Contest

Guess what? Dolly once joined a contest where people dressed up to look like her, and she didn't win! It's a funny story because it shows just how special and unique Dolly's style really is. Even Dolly can't beat how Dolly looks, which just goes to show she's one of a kind.

Favorite Color

Pink is Dolly Parton's favorite color, and it suits her perfectly! Whether she's on stage or walking the red carpet, you can bet there'll be something pink on her. This color matches her fun and lively personality, making everything around her bright and cheerful.

Did you know?

Musical Versatility

At the 2014 Glastonbury Festival, Dolly Parton surprised everyone by playing the saxophone! Most people know her as a singer and songwriter, but she showed that she can play instruments too. This cool moment proves that Dolly loves to keep surprising her fans with new talents.

Influence of the Bible

Dolly Parton's favorite book is the Bible. She reads it often, finding inspiration and guidance for her life and music. Many of her songs reflect the lessons and stories she's learned from the Bible, showing how important her faith is to her and how it shapes everything she does.

Did you know?

Passion for Cooking

Dolly Parton isn't just a music star; she's also fantastic in the kitchen! She loves to cook Southern comfort food and share her recipes with her fans. This way, she gives everyone a little taste of her Tennessee home, making her fans feel like they're part of her family.

Alternative Career as a Doctor

Did you know Dolly Parton once thought about being a doctor? She loves helping people so much that if she hadn't become a famous singer, she might have gone to medical school. Her dream of helping others shows just how caring she is, whether she's on stage or off.

Did you know?

Strong Work Ethic

Dolly Parton is one of the hardest working people in music. She often wakes up at three in the morning to write songs when everything is quiet. This dedication to her music is why she has been able to create so many songs and stay popular for so long. Her hard work really pays off!

Generosity and Helping Others

Dolly Parton has a big heart! She loves helping people who need a hand, and she often does this quietly, without making a big show of it. Whether she's supporting a charity or just doing something nice for someone, Dolly always tries to make the world a better place because she really cares about people.

Did you know?

Butterfly Garden

At her home in Tennessee, Dolly has a beautiful butterfly garden. It's full of colorful butterflies that flutter around, making it a peaceful place for her to relax and get inspired. This special garden shows how much Dolly loves nature and finds beauty in the calm and quiet moments.

No Driver's License

Did you know Dolly Parton doesn't drive? She never got a driver's license because she prefers to have someone else drive her. This way, she can sit back and think up new songs or just enjoy looking out the window without worrying about the road.

Show Off Your Dolly Smarts!

7. In which movie did Dolly Parton star alongside Jane Fonda and Lily Tomlin?

A) "Steel Magnolias"
B) "The Best Little Whorehouse in Texas"
C) "9 to 5"
D) "Rhinestone"

8. What is Dolly Parton's natural hair color?

A) Blonde
B) Red
C) Black
D) Brunette

Answers

7. In which movie did Dolly Parton star alongside Jane Fonda and Lily Tomlin?

A) "Steel Magnolias"
B) "The Best Little Whorehouse in Texas"
C) "9 to 5"
D) "Rhinestone"

8. What is Dolly Parton's natural hair color?

A) Blonde
B) Red
C) Black
D) Brunette

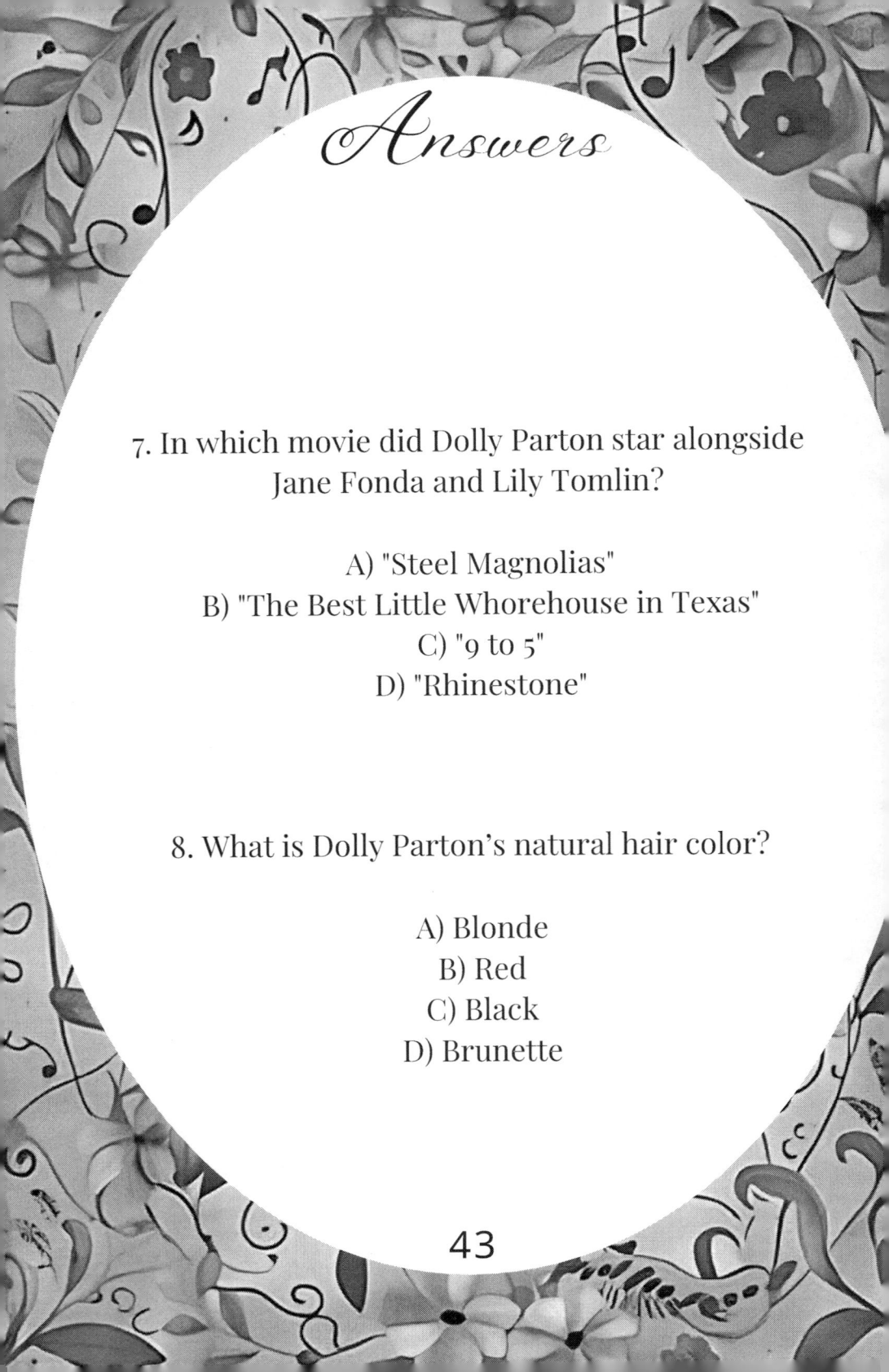

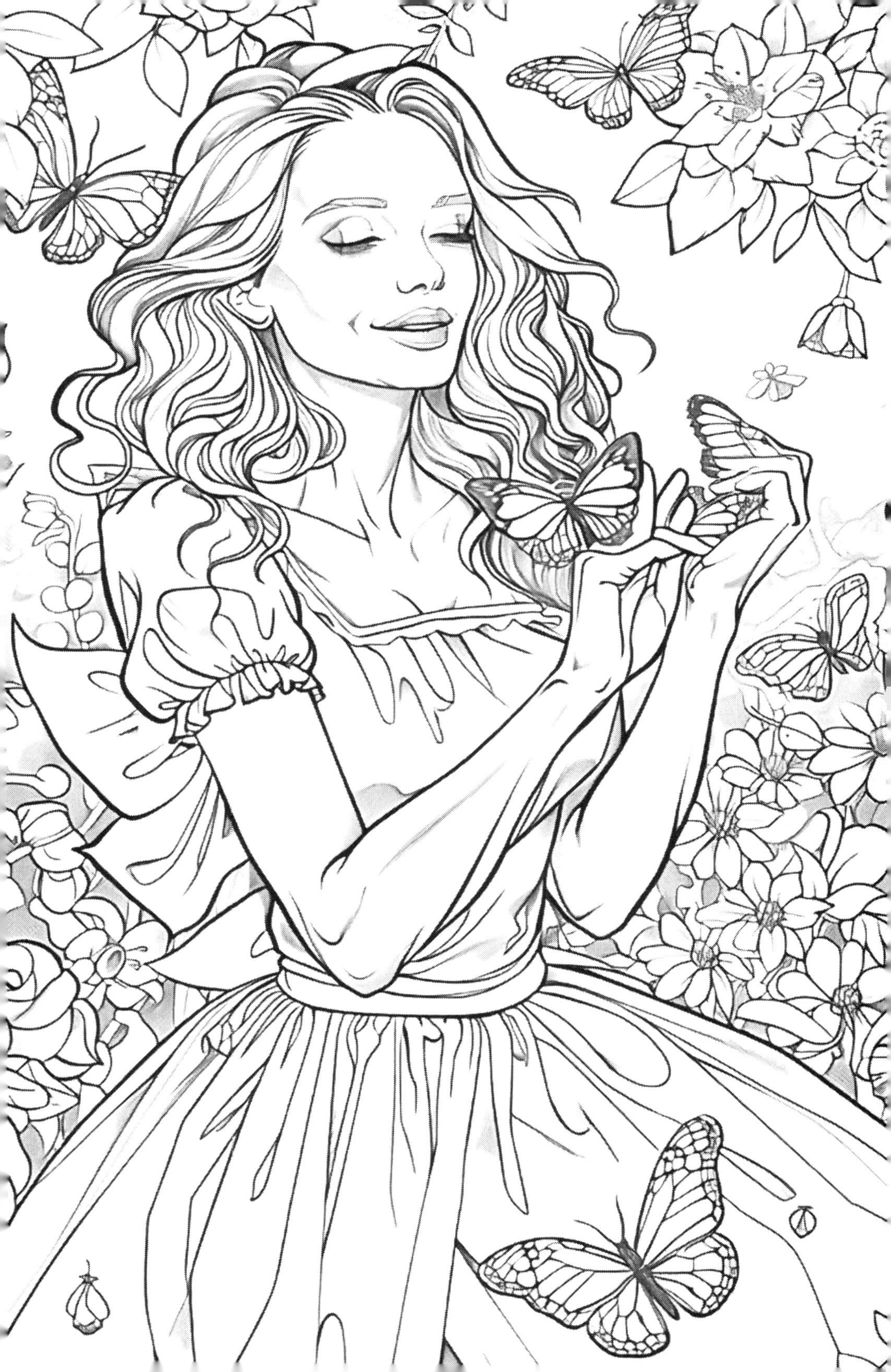

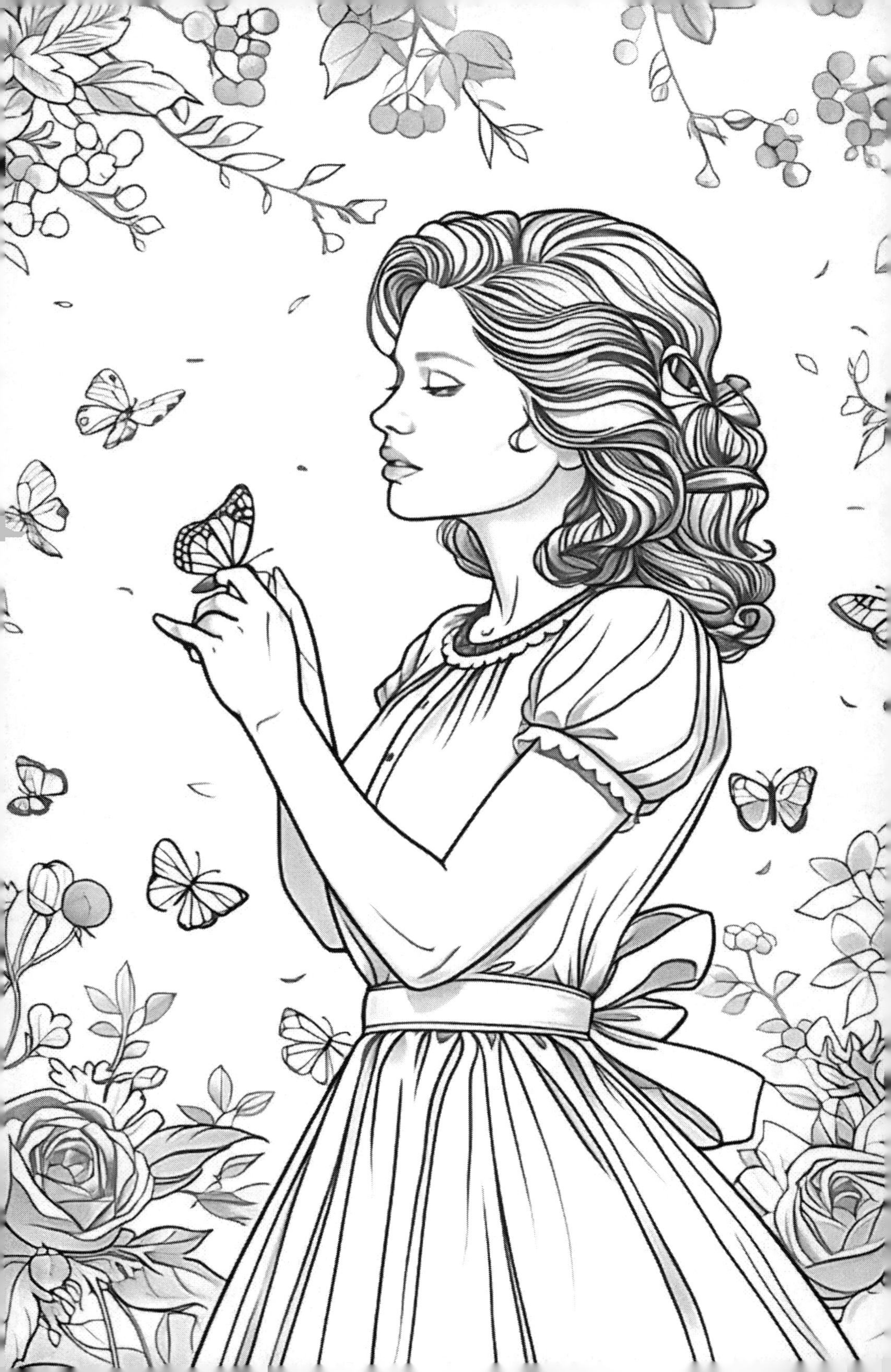

Did you know?

Love for Christmas

Christmas is Dolly's favorite time of the year! She loves it so much that she's made several Christmas albums to share the holiday spirit with everyone. Dolly's Christmas music is filled with joy and the special warmth that makes the holiday season so magical.

Voice as Her Best Asset

Dolly believes that her singing voice is her most special talent. She takes really good care of her voice because it helps her sing all those beautiful songs that people love so much. Her unique voice is one of the reasons she's such a beloved singer all around the world.

Did you know?

Love for Animals

Dolly Parton adores animals! She especially loves dogs and keeps several furry friends as pets. Her deep affection for animals shines through in the way she cares for them, showing just how kind and nurturing she can be. For Dolly, these pets aren't just animals; they're loyal companions who offer endless love and joy.

Skill as a Seamstress

Long before she lit up stages worldwide, Dolly Parton was stitching her own dazzling costumes. With needle and thread in hand, she crafted outfits that sparkled under the spotlight, each piece a perfect reflection of her sparkling personality. This knack for sewing not only saved money but also sewed the seeds of her iconic style that fans adore.

Did you know?

Early Riser for Songwriting

While the world is still asleep, Dolly is up with the sunrise, penning her next hit song. These quiet morning hours are her secret to success, providing a calm space to let her creativity flow. This disciplined start to her day shows just how dedicated Dolly is to her music, crafting songs that touch hearts across the globe.

Signature Fragrance

Dolly Parton's signature fragrance, "Dolly – Scent from Above," is as delightful and enchanting as she is. This special perfume captures the essence of her sparkling charm and love for all things beautiful. Just a spritz, and it's like carrying a piece of Dolly's magic everywhere you go, reminding you to always keep your spirits high and your heart joyful.

Did you know?

Advocate for Literacy and Education

Dolly Parton isn't just about music; she's passionate about books too! She works tirelessly to get books into the hands of kids everywhere, believing that reading opens new worlds. Through her Imagination Library, she helps ignite imaginations and dreams, proving that books are keys to a treasure chest of knowledge and wonder.

Fear of Flying

Even superstars have fears, and Dolly Parton is no exception. She's not a fan of flying in airplanes. Instead, she loves to travel on buses, which she finds snug and soothing. This way, she can watch the world go by at her own pace, which really suits her down-to-earth nature.

Did you know?

Favorite Movie

"The Wizard of Oz" isn't just a movie to Dolly; it's a treasure chest of lessons about bravery, adventure, and the magic of home. Ever since she was a little girl, this movie has held a special place in her heart, inspiring some of the heartfelt themes in her music and life.

Songwriting and Dreams

Imagine dreaming up a song! That's exactly what happens with Dolly. Often, new melodies and lyrics come to her in her dreams, showing just how deep her creativity runs. When she wakes up, she turns these dream snippets into beautiful music, adding a touch of magic to her songs.

Show Off Your Dolly Smarts!

9. What special item does Dolly have a whole room dedicated to in her house?

A) Shoes
B) Hats
C) Wigs
D) Jewelry

10. Which book did Dolly Parton write for children, teaching them about emotions and colors?

A) "I Am a Rainbow"
B) "Color My World"
C) "Feelings and Colors"
D) "Dolly's Color Book"

Answers

9. What special item does Dolly have a whole room dedicated to in her house?

A) Shoes
B) Hats
C) Wigs
D) Jewelry

10. Which book did Dolly Parton write for children, teaching them about emotions and colors?

A) "I Am a Rainbow"
B) "Color My World"
C) "Feelings and Colors"
D) "Dolly's Color Book"

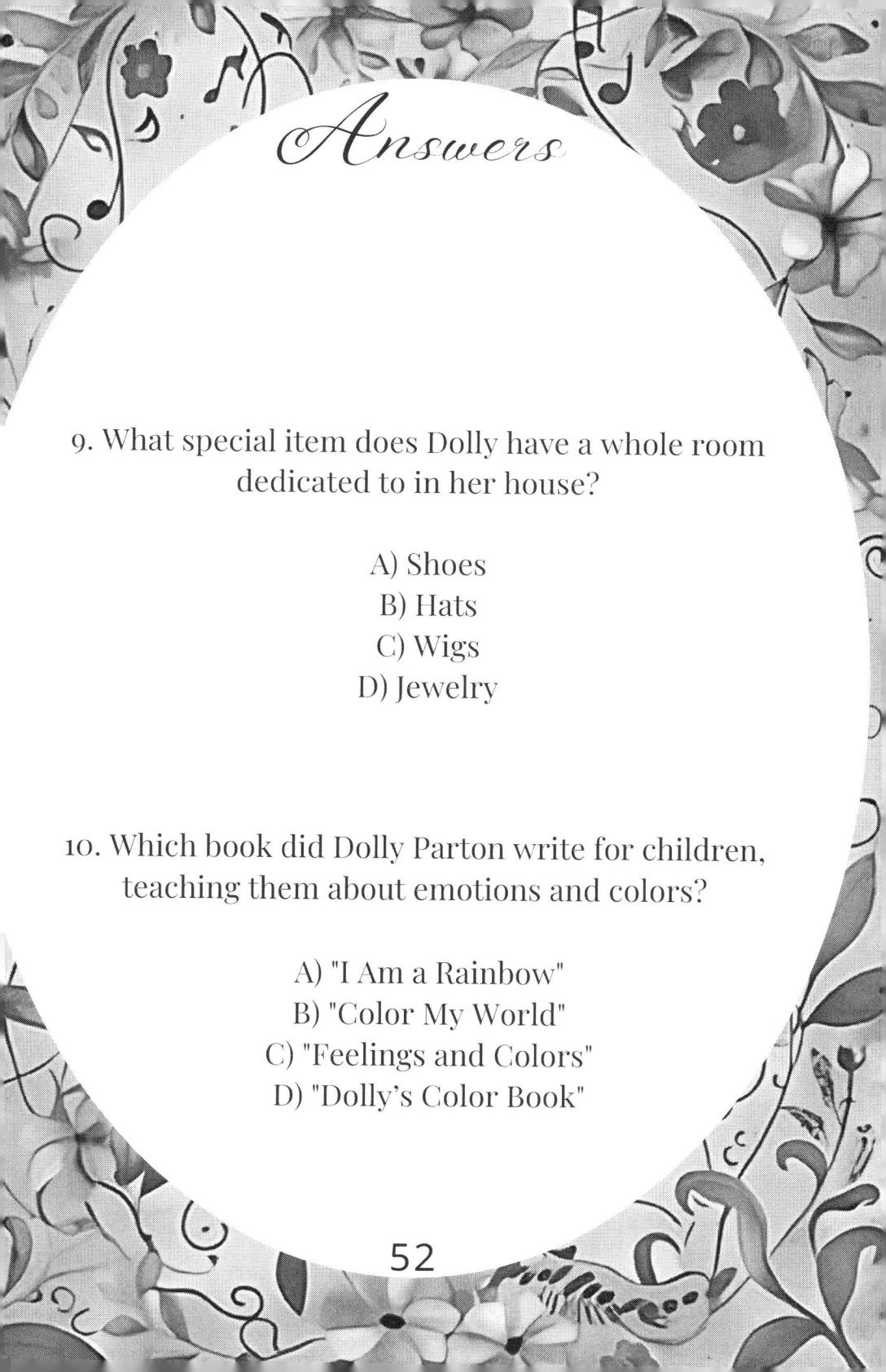

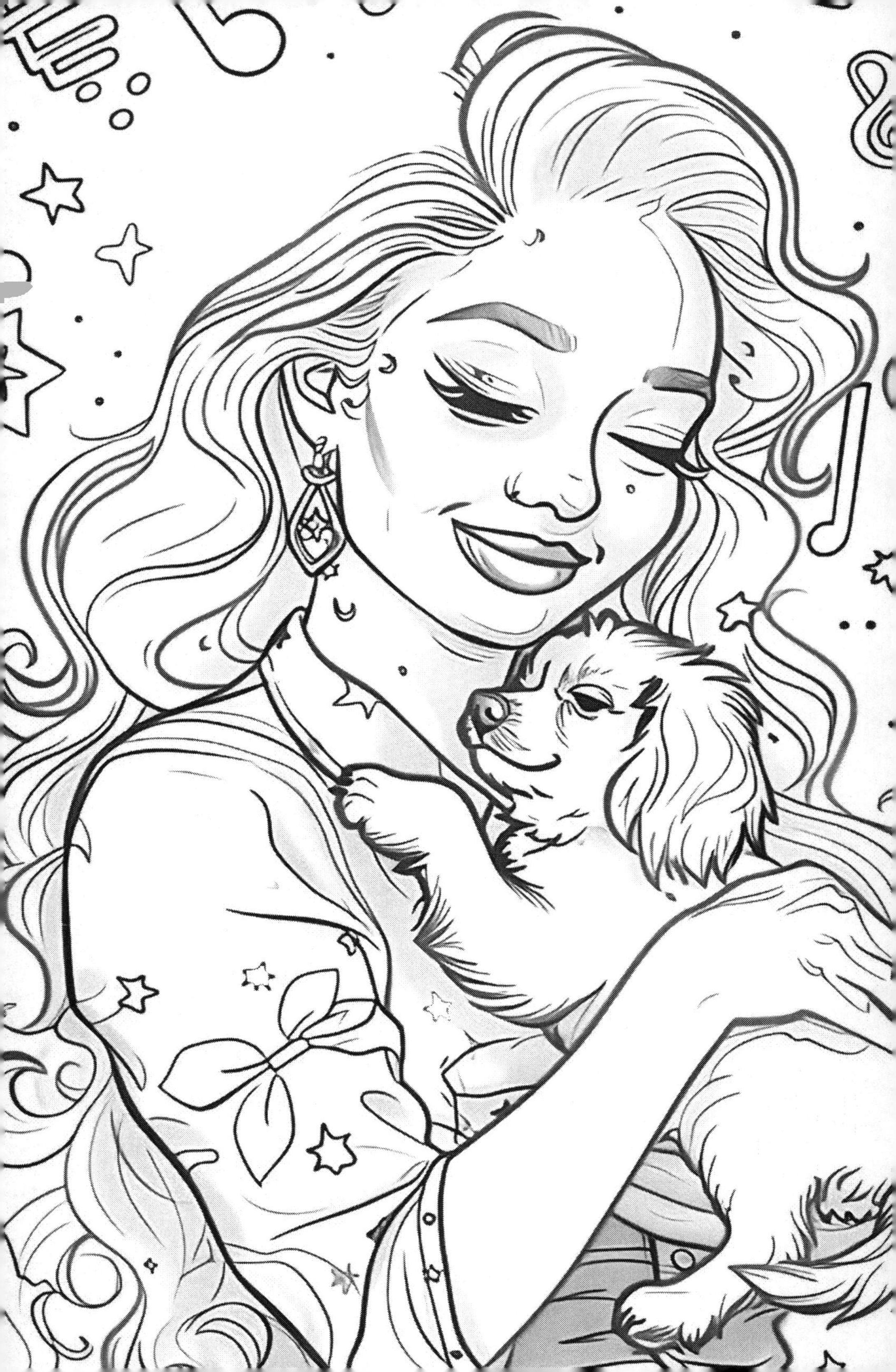

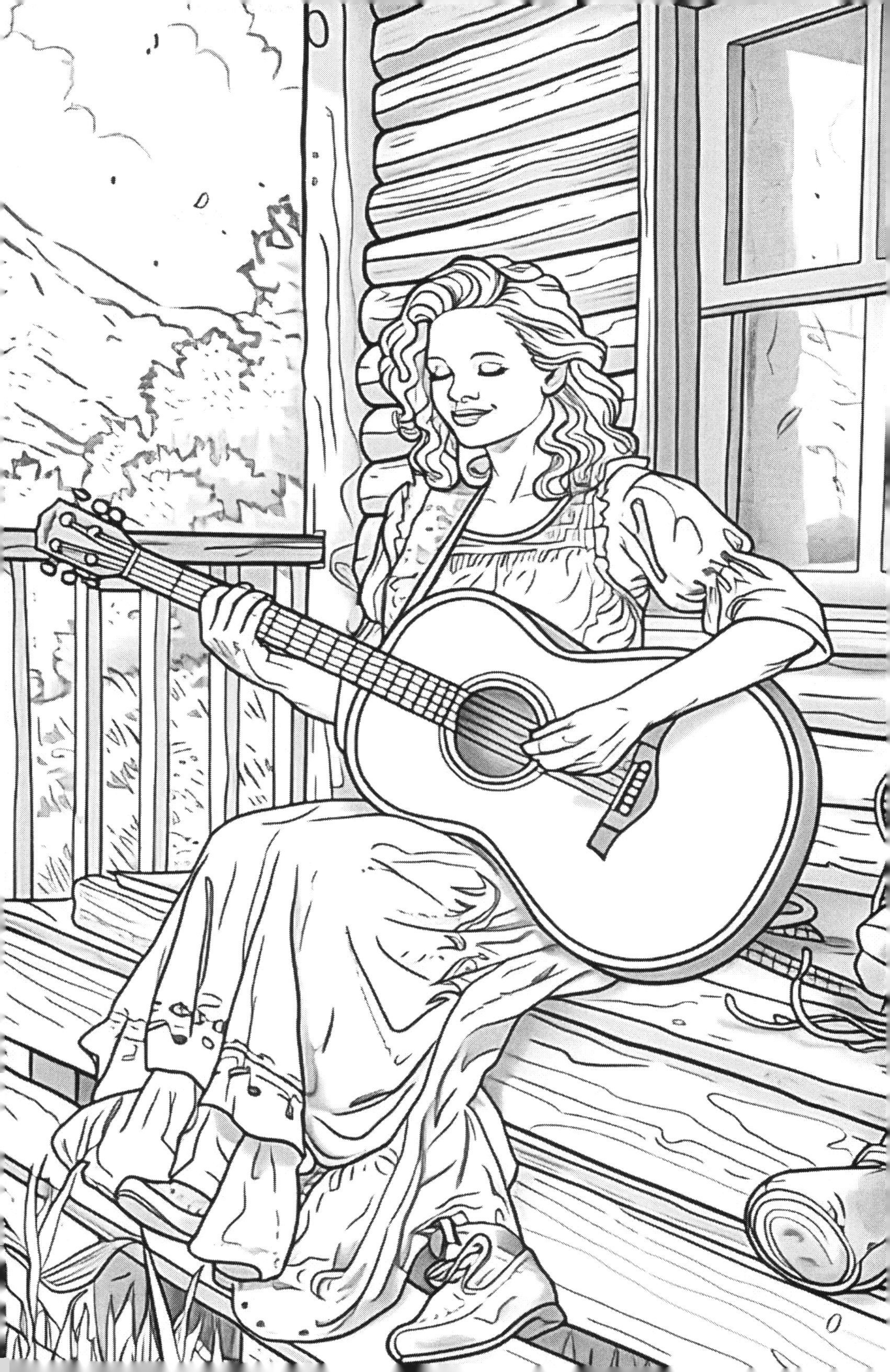

Did you know?

Collecting Butterflies

Dolly adores butterflies so much that she collects them! For her, these delicate creatures symbolize freedom and beauty, and she surrounds herself with their images in her garden and outfits. Her love for butterflies shows how much beauty and grace influence her life and work.

Homemade Christmas Gifts

Every Christmas, Dolly gets busy with glue, glitter, and scissors, making gifts for her loved ones. She believes that a gift you make is a gift from the heart, showing her thoughtful and loving spirit. This festive tradition is one of the ways Dolly shares joy and shows her family and friends just how much they mean to her.

Did you know?

Love for Gardening

Dolly Parton treasures her time in the garden. With her hands in the soil and surrounded by blooms, she feels a deep joy and peace. Gardening gives her a chance to help things grow, and it fills her with pride to see her flowers and plants flourish under her care.

Love for Classic Country Music

When it comes to music, Dolly Parton holds a special place in her heart for the classics. Legends like Loretta Lynn and George Jones not only tune her strings but also inspire her own music. Their songs connect her to the deep and rich traditions of country music, which shape her own melodies and stories.

Did you know?

Custom Tour Bus

Imagine traveling the country in your own rolling home. That's exactly what Dolly does with her custom tour bus! It's like a cozy little house on wheels, complete with all the comfy spots she needs. This bus makes sure she has a slice of home, no matter where her music takes her.

Passion for Painting

When she's not making music, Dolly Parton loves to paint. Brush in hand, she brings colors to life on canvas, expressing her emotions and thoughts through her art. Painting is just another way Dolly shares her incredible creativity, showing the world her talents don't just stop at music.

Did you know?

Favorite Snack

For Dolly Parton, nothing beats snacking on popcorn while watching a good movie. This simple treat speaks to her love of life's simple pleasures. It's a small joy that reminds us all to cherish the comfy, quiet moments that make life sweet.

Natural Hair Color

Did you know Dolly Parton wasn't always the blonde superstar we see today? She's actually a natural brunette! Dolly started dyeing her hair blonde when she was a teenager, and that bright, sunny color has become a big part of her sparkling image.

Did you know?

Interest in Interior Design

Dolly loves making places look beautiful, not just with her clothes but also in her home. She has a real knack for interior design, filling her rooms with colors and decorations that show off her unique style. It's like walking into a room full of Dolly's personality—comfortable, colorful, and glamorous all at once!

Favorite Dessert

When it comes to sweets, Dolly's all-time favorite is banana pudding. This creamy, dreamy dessert is a classic in the South, where Dolly grew up. It's not just delicious; it also brings back memories of her childhood and the tasty treats she enjoyed with her family.

Show Off Your Dolly Smarts!

11. At what age did Dolly Parton first perform at the Grand Ole Opry?

    A) 10
    B) 13
    C) 15
    D) 18

12. What is Dolly Parton's favorite flower?

    A) Daisy
    B) Rose
    C) Tulip
    D) Sunflower

Answers

11. At what age did Dolly Parton first perform at the Grand Ole Opry?

A) 10
B) 13
C) 15
D) 18

12. What is Dolly Parton's favorite flower?

A) Daisy
B) Rose
C) Tulip
D) Sunflower

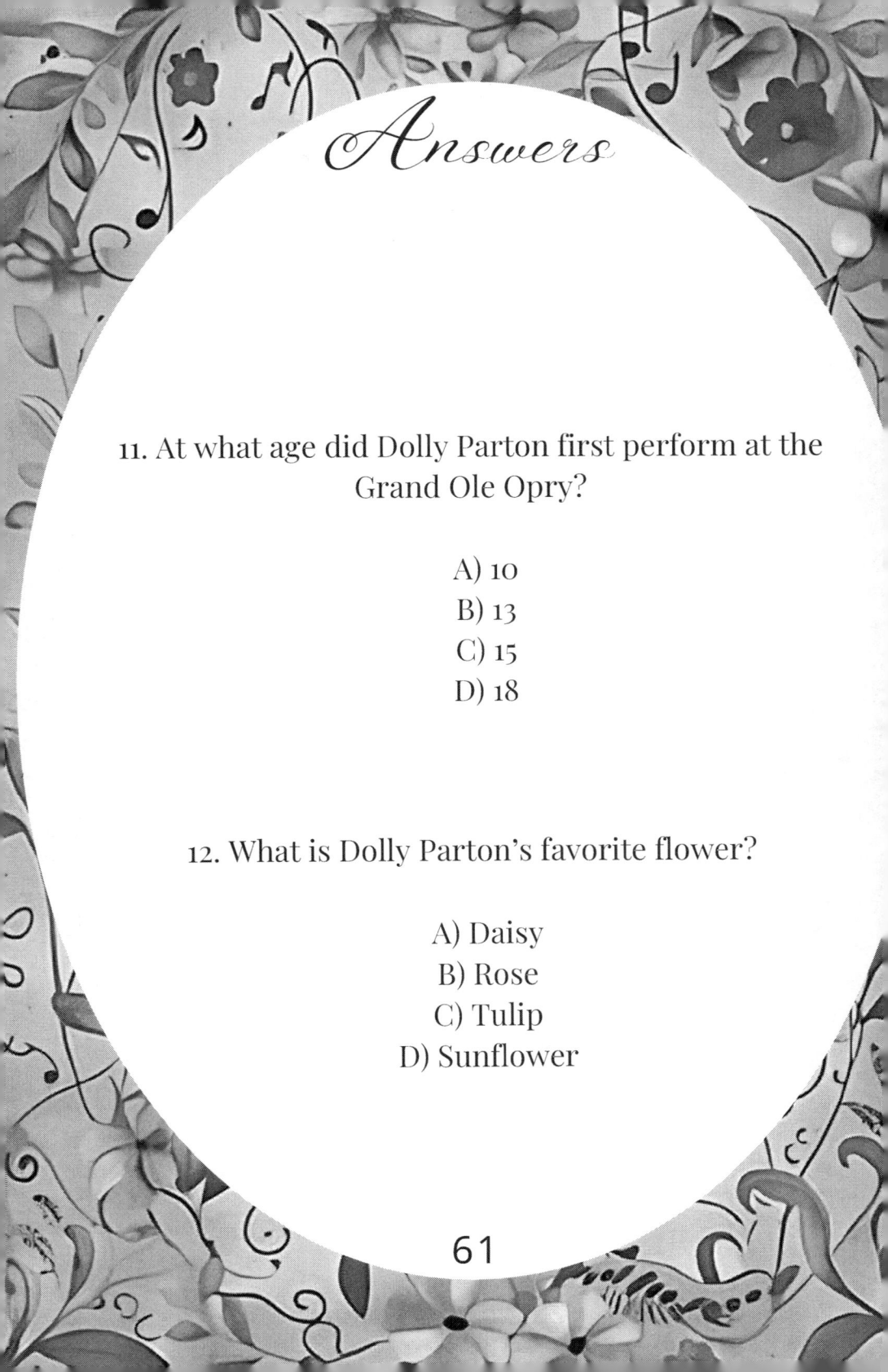

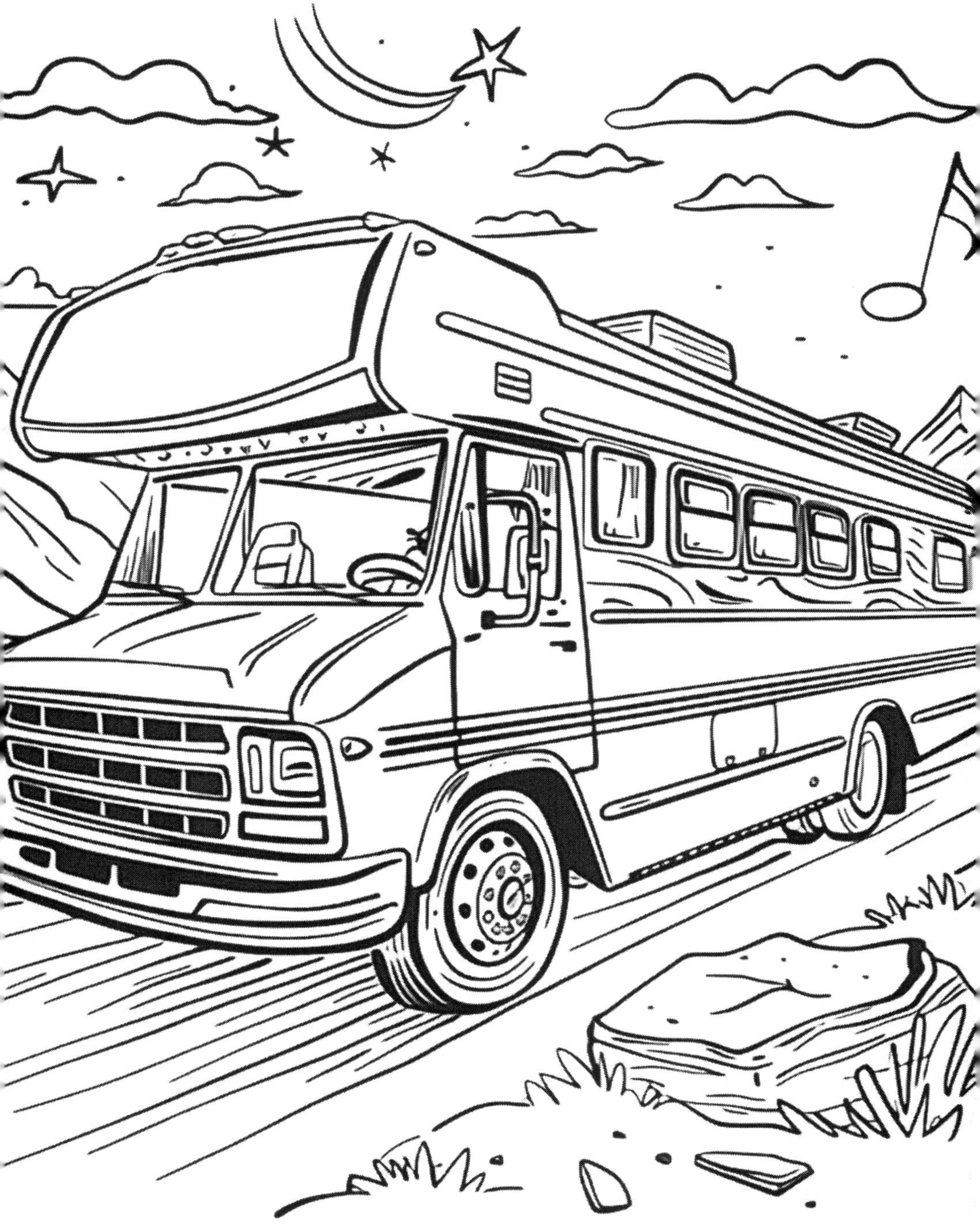

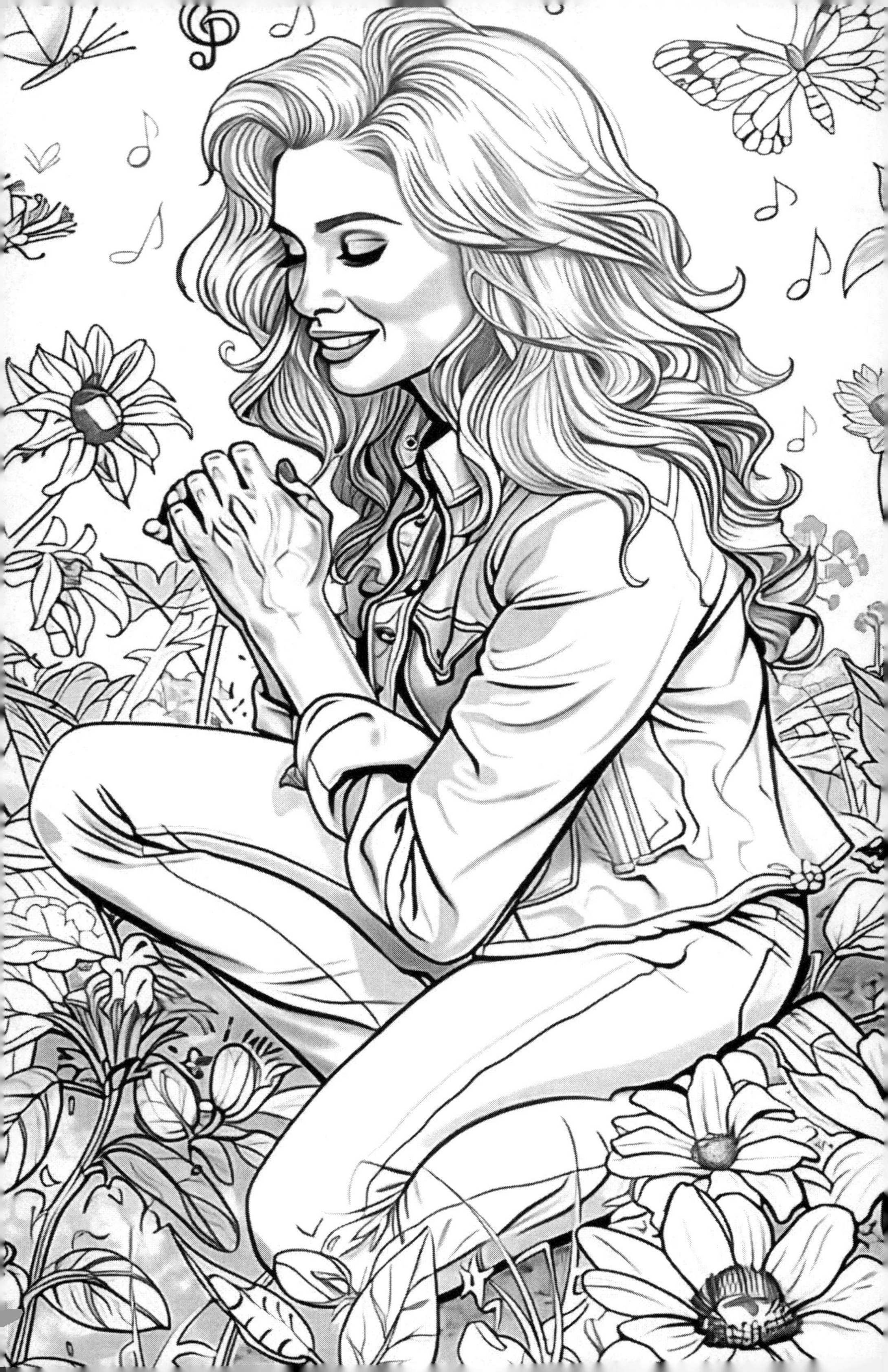

Did you know?

Philanthropy in Education

Dolly Parton believes that every child should have a chance to learn and dream big. That's why she's so passionate about education. Through scholarships and support for educational programs, Dolly helps open doors for kids and teens, giving them the tools they need to succeed and make their dreams come true.

Time on the Porch

One of Dolly's favorite places is her porch in Tennessee. There, surrounded by the quiet beauty of nature, she takes time to sit back and relax. It's a perfect spot for thinking, dreaming up new songs, or just enjoying a quiet afternoon. This special porch time helps Dolly stay connected to her roots and find peace in her busy life.

Did you know?

Belief in Angels

Dolly Parton feels a special connection to angels, believing they watch over her and guide her through life. This belief brings her comfort and shows how deeply she values her spiritual side. For Dolly, angels are not just imaginary; they are a real presence that fills her days with hope and light.

Fishing Hobby

Cast a line into the water with Dolly, and you'll find one of her favorite ways to relax—fishing! She learned this peaceful pastime from her father when she was a little girl. It's a time for her to enjoy the quiet of nature and remember the simple joys of her Tennessee childhood.

Did you know?

Extensive Wig Collection

Imagine a closet filled with over 300 wigs, each one a different color or style. That's a peek into Dolly's dazzling world! She loves to mix up her look with these wigs, making each public appearance a new and exciting reveal. This collection is not just fashion; it's a fun part of how she expresses her vibrant personality.

Favorite Season

When the leaves start to turn, Dolly Parton's heart fills with joy. Autumn is her favorite time of year because it paints her beloved Smoky Mountains in spectacular colors. This season brings back sweet memories of her childhood, making her feel like she's walking through those hills all over again.

Did you know?

Naming Her Wigs

Dolly doesn't just wear wigs; she brings them to life by giving each one a name and a personality. This fun habit turns her collection into a gallery of characters, each with its own story. It's a whimsical way that shows Dolly's playful and creative spirit in everything she does.

Sense of Humor

Dolly Parton is as famous for her laughter as she is for her music. She often pokes fun at herself and her glamorous image, which makes everyone chuckle along with her. This wonderful sense of humor helps her stay down-to-earth and connects her with fans who love her not just as a star, but as a genuinely funny and humble person.

Did you know?

Favorite Flower

Roses are Dolly's favorite flowers, and it's easy to see why. They represent love and beauty, which are themes you can find in many of her heartfelt songs. Dolly's choice of roses reflects her romantic side and her love for things that are timeless and beautiful.

Songwriting on the Porch Swing

There's a special place where Dolly feels the music flow freely—the porch swing at her home. Sitting there, surrounded by the quiet beauty of nature, Dolly writes some of her most touching songs. This peaceful spot is where she connects with her thoughts and lets her creativity soar.

Show Off Your Dolly Smarts!

13. What nickname does Dolly Parton often use to refer to herself?

A) Backwoods Barbie
B) Country Queen
C) Mountain Girl
D) Southern Star

14. What was the name of the TV show where Dolly Parton made regular appearances as a child?

A) "The Porter Wagoner Show"
B) "The Cas Walker Show"
C) "Hee Haw"
D) "Dolly"

Answers

13. What nickname does Dolly Parton often use to refer to herself?

    A) Backwoods Barbie
    B) Country Queen
    C) Mountain Girl
    D) Southern Star

14. What was the name of the TV show where Dolly Parton made regular appearances as a child?

    A) "The Porter Wagoner Show"
    B) "The Cas Walker Show"
    C) "Hee Haw"
    D) "Dolly"

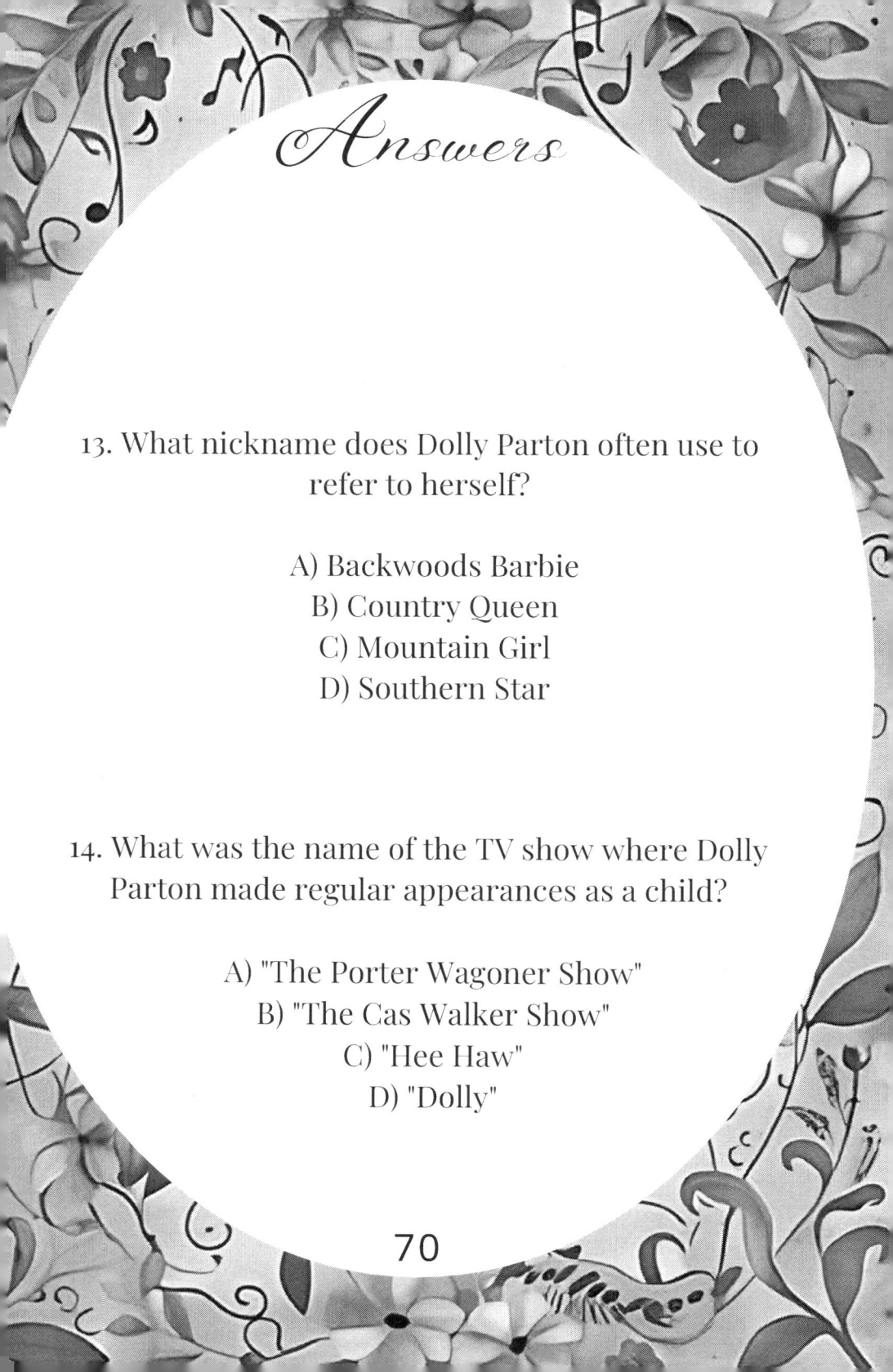

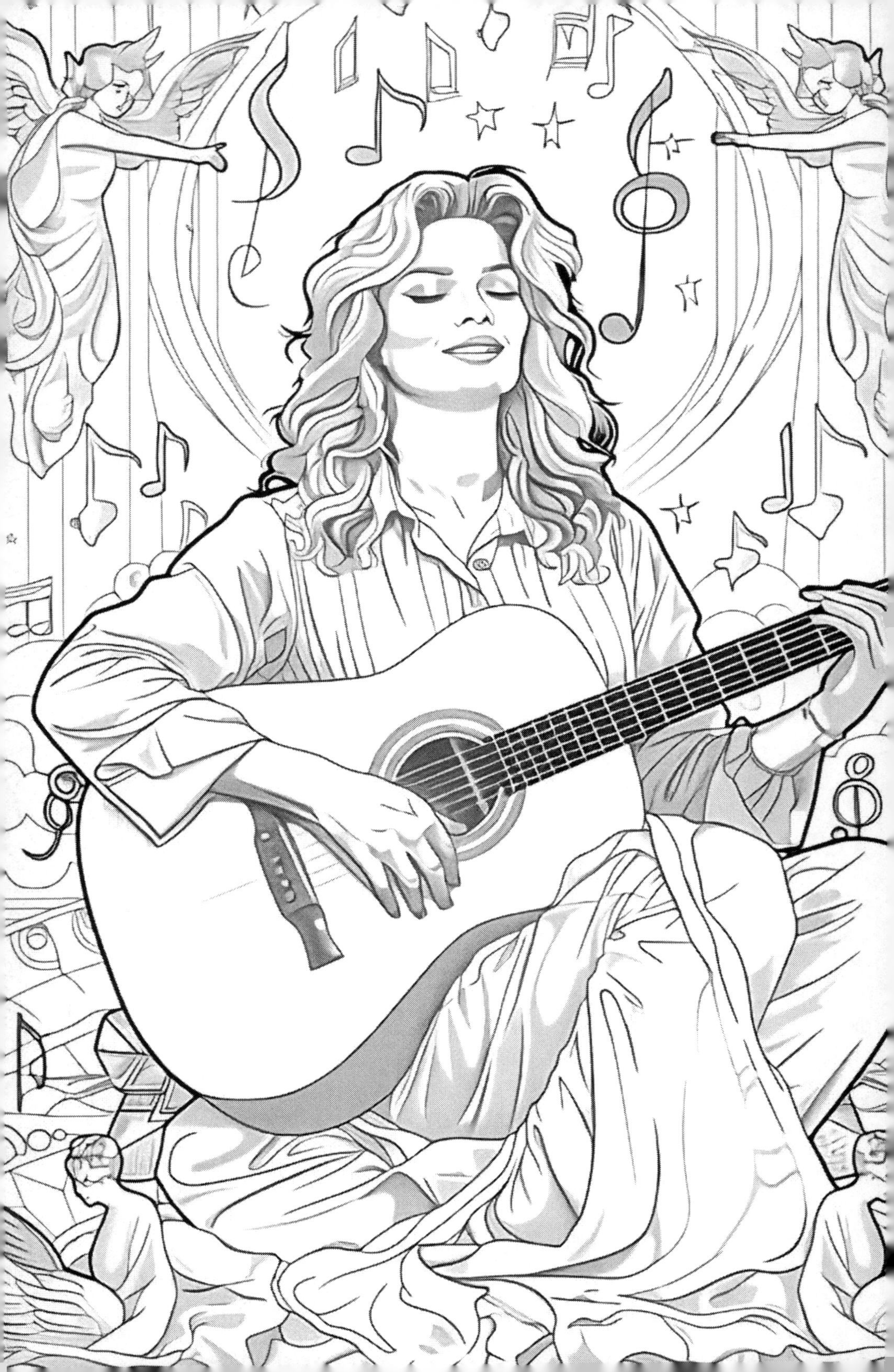

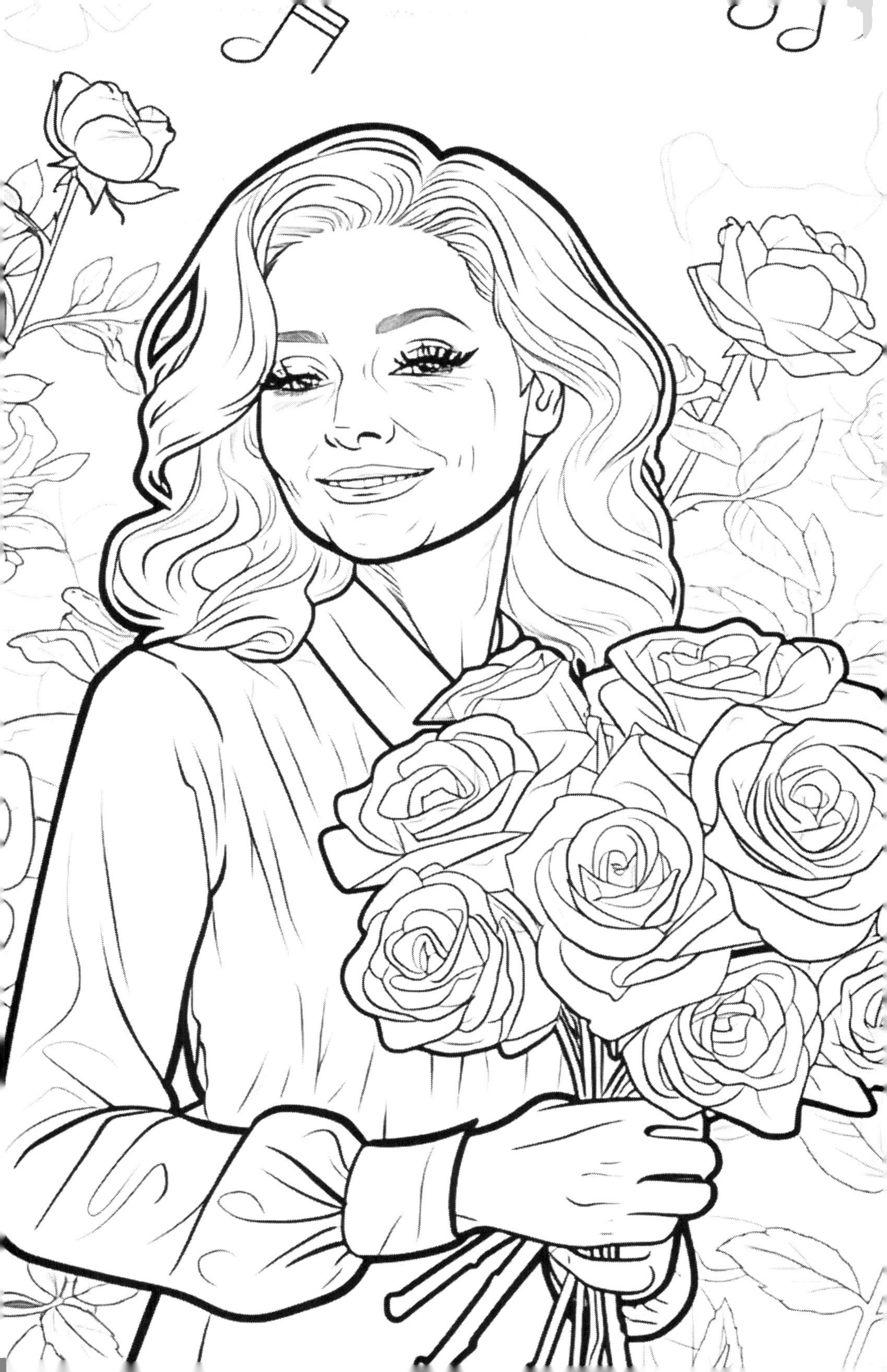

Did you know?

Country Music Association Awards

Dolly Parton's trophy shelf is filled with 11 Country Music Association Awards, shining proof of her incredible talent. These awards, including the coveted Entertainer of the Year, highlight just how much Dolly has achieved and how deeply she's influenced the world of country music.

Writing "Jolene" and "I Will Always Love You"

Imagine writing not just one, but two legendary songs in a single day! That's what Dolly Parton did with "Jolene" and "I Will Always Love You." This incredible achievement shows how magically her mind spins emotions and stories into songs that the whole world loves and sings.

Did you know?

Dolly's House in Tennessee

Step into Dolly's house in Tennessee and you'll find a magical place filled with keepsakes from her amazing career. Every corner tells a story of songs, shows, and sparkling moments from her journey in music and movies.

Spiritual Songs

Dolly's music often touches the soul, especially her gospel songs that reflect her deep spiritual beliefs. Through these songs, she shares her faith and brings comfort and joy to her listeners, showing another layer of her heartfelt artistry.

Did you know?

Distinctive Guitar Playing

Dolly has a unique trick when playing guitar—she uses her acrylic nails as picks! This clever technique helps create her signature sound, blending traditional skills with her own sparkling flair.

Charitable Work During Disasters

When trouble strikes, Dolly Parton is always ready to help. She has donated generously to help people affected by wildfires and other disasters, especially in her beloved Tennessee. Her actions show her big heart and deep roots in her community.

Did you know?

Wig Storage Room

Dolly's dazzling wigs have their own room in her house! She has a whole collection of different styles and colors, each wig ready to add some extra sparkle to her look. This special room is a fun glimpse into how Dolly creates her famous, fabulous appearances.

Love for Classic Movies

Dolly Parton adores classic films, and she holds a special place in her heart for "Steel Magnolias," where she starred as the charming Truvy Jones. Her love for these movies isn't just about the acting; it's about the powerful stories they tell, connecting her deeper to the magic of the film world.

Did you know?

Creativity in the Morning

Early in the morning, while the world is still quiet, Dolly feels her creative spark ignite. This is her favorite time to write songs and dream up new ideas. In these peaceful morning hours, some of her best-loved songs have come to life, showing how much she cherishes this serene time to create.

Favorite Personal Clothing

Among Dolly's treasured possessions is a colorful coat her mother made for her when she was little, which inspired her touching song "Coat of Many Colors." This coat is more than just fabric; it's a reminder of her modest beginnings and the warmth and love of her family, echoing the heartfelt themes in her music.

Show Off Your Dolly Smarts!

15. What unique writing spot does Dolly Parton have on her property?

A) Treehouse
B) Camper trailer
C) Boat house
D) Gazebo

16. Which of these songs did Dolly Parton write in a single day along with "I Will Always Love You"?

A) "Jolene"
B) "9 to 5"
C) "Here You Come Again"
D) "Islands in the Stream"

Answers

15. What unique writing spot does Dolly Parton have on her property?

   A) Treehouse
   B) Camper trailer
   C) Boat house
   D) Gazebo

16. Which of these songs did Dolly Parton write in a single day along with "I Will Always Love You"?

   A) "Jolene"
   B) "9 to 5"
   C) "Here You Come Again"
   D) "Islands in the Stream"

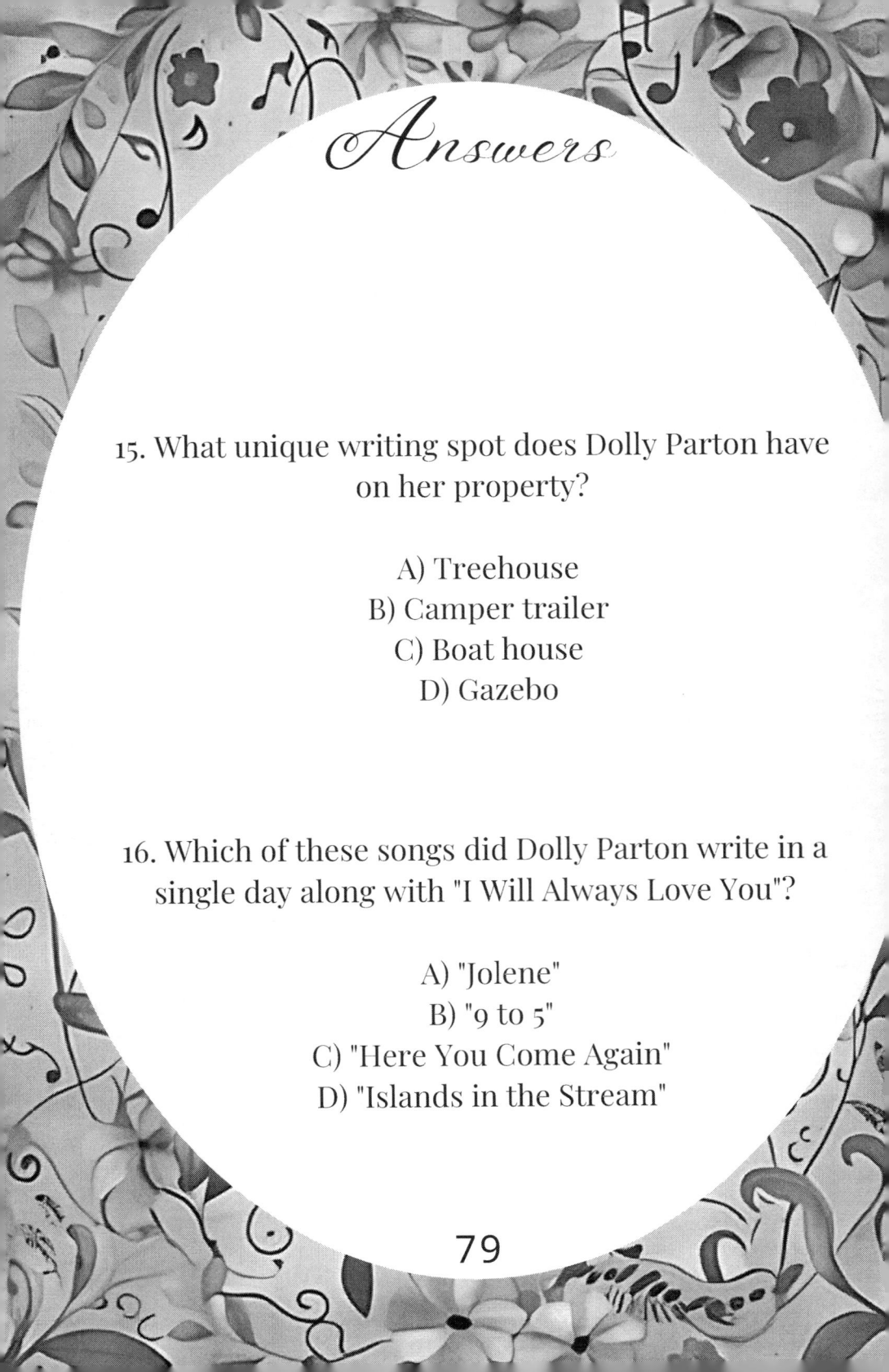

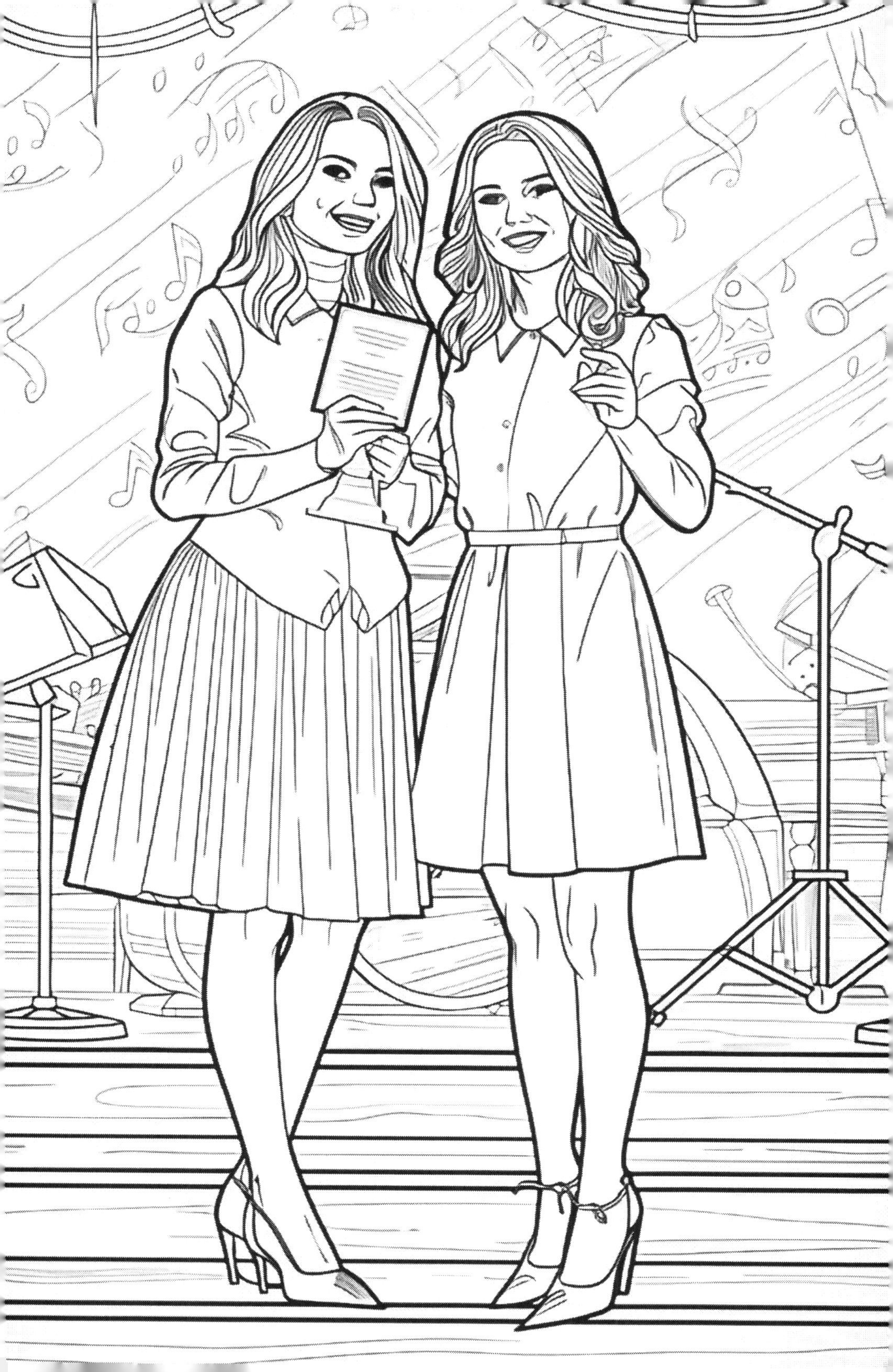

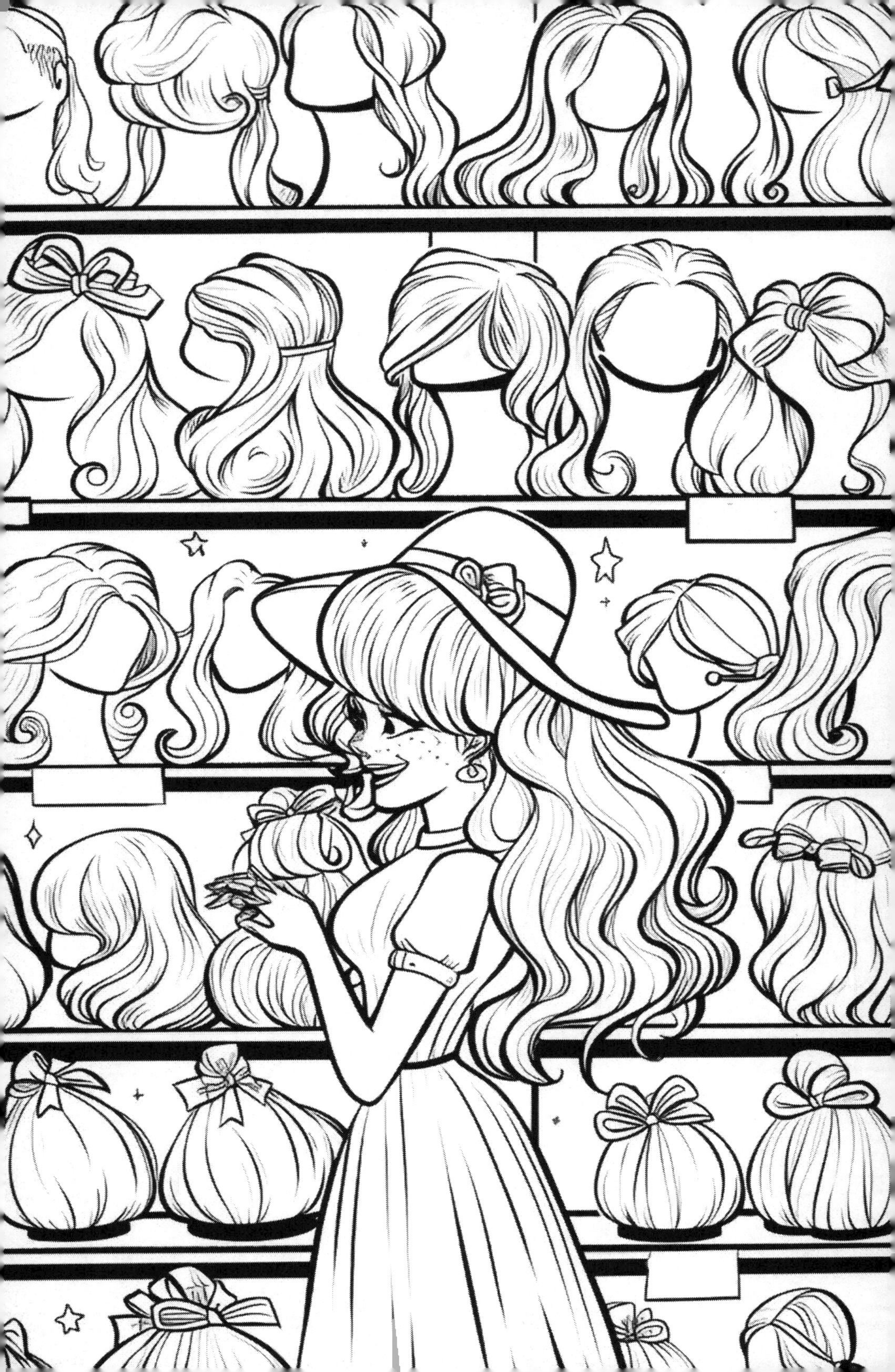

Did you know?

Environmental Advocacy

Dolly is deeply committed to protecting the environment, especially the beautiful Great Smoky Mountains where she grew up. Her environmental work shows her dedication to keeping nature pristine and lovely for everyone to enjoy, just as she did as a child.

Favorite Performance at the Grand Ole Opry

One of Dolly's most cherished memories is singing at the Grand Ole Opry when she was just 13 years old. Stepping onto that legendary stage marked a pivotal moment in her early career, setting the stage for her incredible journey in country music.

Did you know?

Fond Childhood Memory

Among Dolly's treasured memories is baking apple dumplings with her mother. This sweet recollection is filled with warmth and love, echoing the simple joys of her childhood. These moments spent cooking in the kitchen not only nurtured her but also strengthened the family bonds that deeply influence her music and life.

Connection to Tennessee Roots

Dolly Parton may be a global superstar, but her heart remains in Tennessee. She cherishes her Smoky Mountain upbringing, which continues to inspire her songs, charity work, and the values she holds dear. Her deep love for her home state is woven through every part of her life, keeping her grounded no matter how far her fame reaches.

Did you know?

Early Musical Exposure on Radio

From a very young age, Dolly was singing on local radio in East Tennessee. By the time she was ten, she was a regular on "The Cas Walker Show." These early performances on radio and TV were crucial in shaping her musical talent and confidence, paving the way for her legendary career in music.

Meeting Husband Carl Dean

Dolly's love story began in an unexpected place—a Nashville laundromat, where she met her future husband, Carl Dean, on her very first day in the city. They married in 1966 and have since enjoyed a strong and private relationship, a quiet constant in the whirlwind of her public life. Their enduring partnership is a testament to their deep love and mutual respect.

Did you know?

Dolly's Theme Park Rides

At Dollywood, her theme park in Tennessee, Dolly has some rides inspired by her own life. One of the most popular rides is the "Wild Eagle," a thrilling roller coaster that lets you soar through the air, just like how Dolly's music soars into our hearts. Kids and families love the fun and excitement of Dollywood's attractions.

Record-Breaking Album Sales

Dolly Parton has sold over 100 million records worldwide! That's more than enough albums to give one to every person in a big country. This amazing achievement shows just how much people all around the world love and enjoy her music.

Did you know?

Signature Butterfly Tattoo

Dolly has a small butterfly tattoo that she keeps mostly hidden. Butterflies are special to her because they represent beauty, transformation, and freedom. This little tattoo is a personal symbol of the things she values most.

Guest-Starring on TV Shows

Dolly Parton has made guest appearances on many popular TV shows, including "Hannah Montana," where she played Aunt Dolly. Fans loved seeing her in this fun role, especially because her real-life goddaughter, Miley Cyrus, starred in the show!

Show Off Your Dolly Smarts!

17. What year was Dolly Parton born?

   A) 1940
   B) 1942
   C) 1946
   D) 1950

18. In which state is Dolly Parton's Dollywood theme park located?

   A) Kentucky
   B) Tennessee
   C) North Carolina
   D) Georgia

Answers

17. What year was Dolly Parton born?

   A) 1940
   B) 1942
   C) 1946
   D) 1950

18. In which state is Dolly Parton's Dollywood theme park located?

   A) Kentucky
   B) Tennessee
   C) North Carolina
   D) Georgia

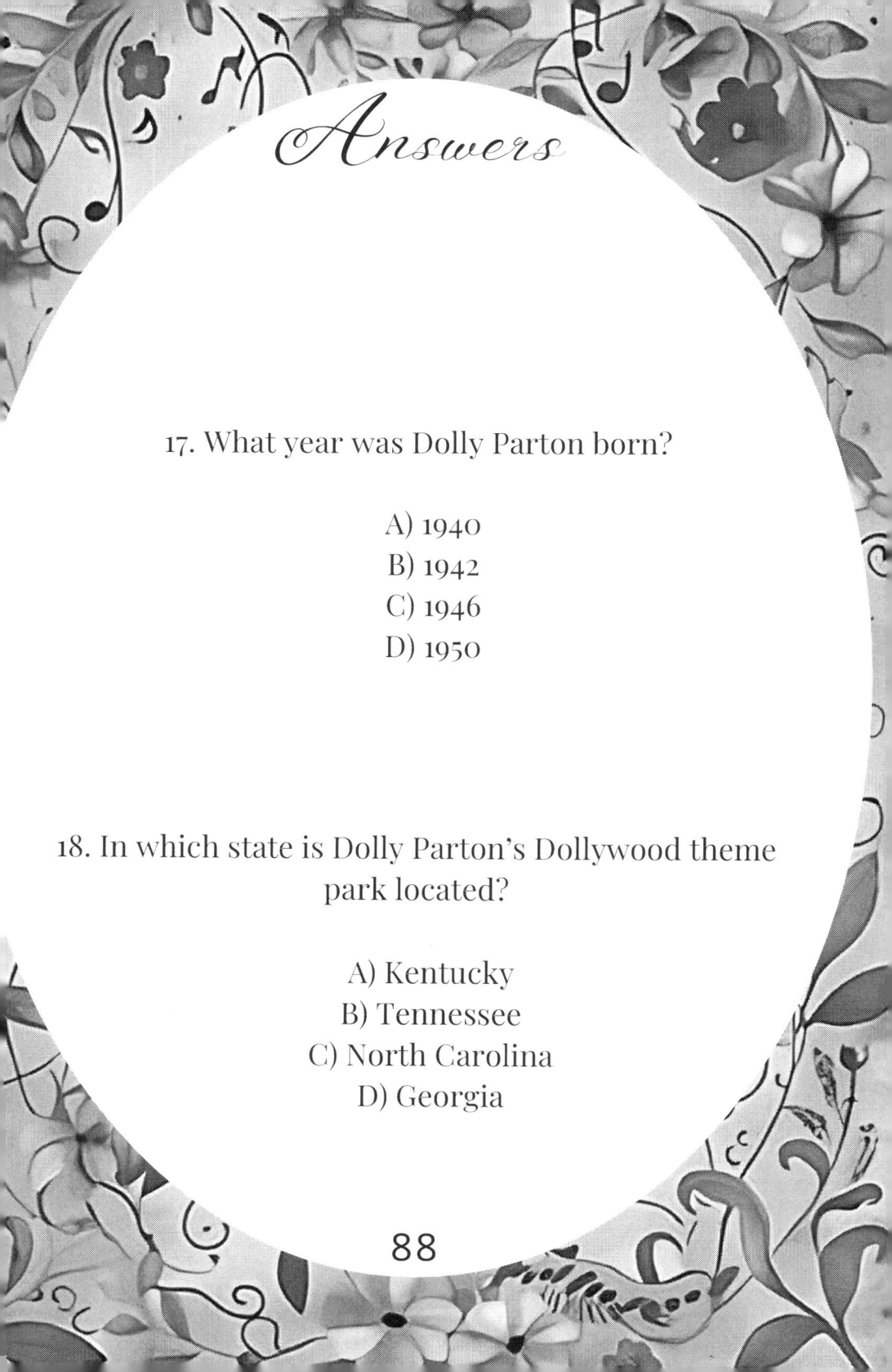

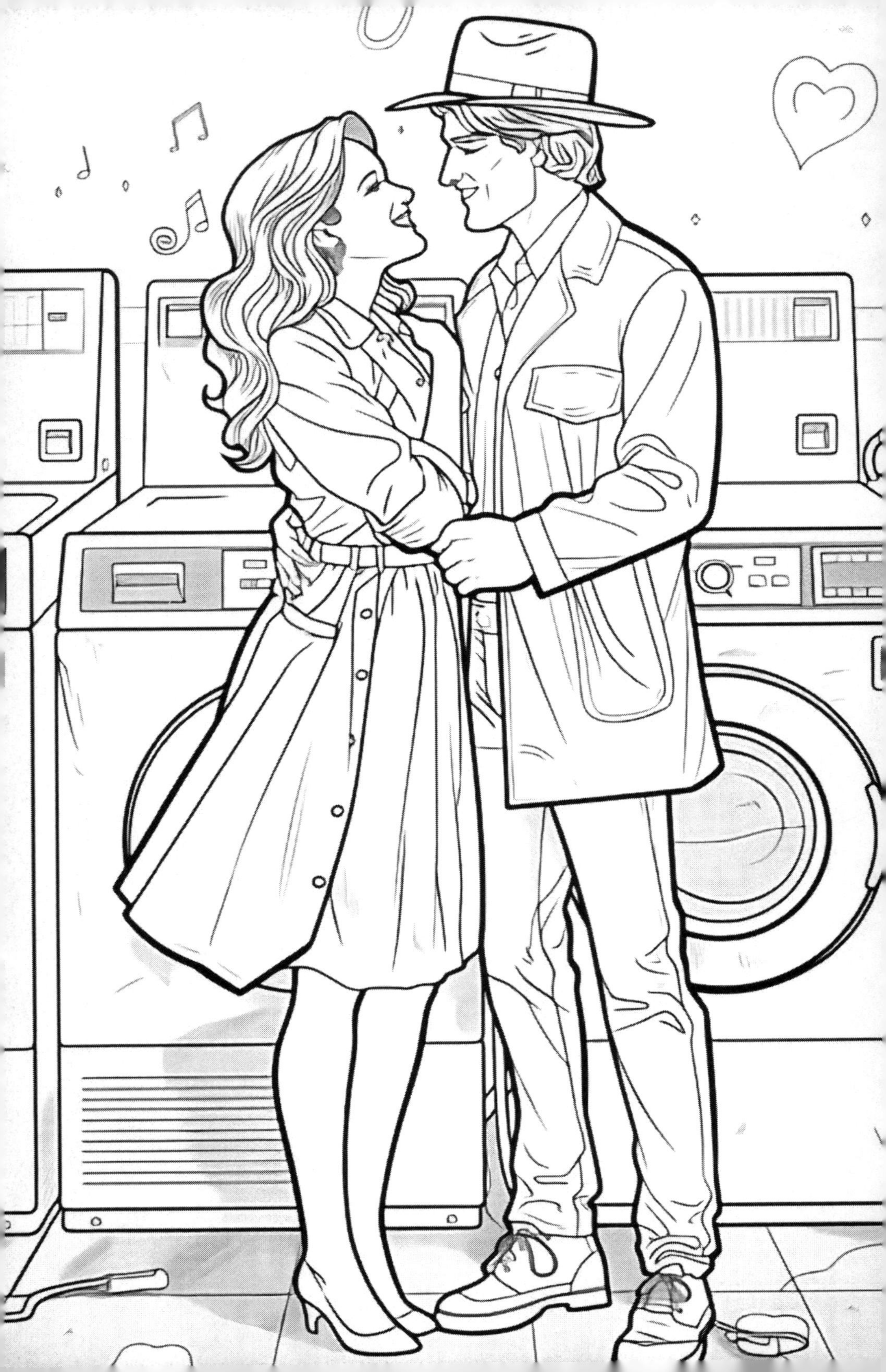

Did you know?

Playing Multiple Instruments

Dolly is not just a fantastic singer; she can also play several instruments. She's talented with the guitar, banjo, piano, and even the autoharp! Her ability to play these instruments adds depth and variety to her music, making it even more special.

Inspirational Quotes

Dolly Parton is known for her wise and funny quotes. One of her most famous sayings is, "If you want the rainbow, you gotta put up with the rain." This quote teaches us that we have to go through tough times to enjoy the good ones.

Extended Trivia!

19. What did Dolly Parton name her signature fragrance?

A) "Dolly's Dream"
B) "Butterfly Kiss"
C) "Scent from Above"
D) "Mountain Magic"

20. Which role did Dolly Parton play in the movie "Steel Magnolias"?

A) M'Lynn Eatenton
B) Shelby Eatenton
C) Truvy Jones
D) Clairee Belcher

21. What is the name of Dolly Parton's husband?

A) Carl Dean
B) Kenny Rogers
C) Porter Wagoner
D) Johnny Cash

Extended Trivia!

22. What is Dolly Parton's favorite snack?

   A) Popcorn
   B) Cookies
   C) Chips
   D) Candy

23. Which famous rock star did Dolly Parton say she'd love to duet with?

   A) Mick Jagger
   B) Paul McCartney
   C) Bruce Springsteen
   D) Elton John

24. What is the name of Dolly Parton's theme park ride inspired by her music career?

   A) "Wild Eagle"
   B) "Thunderhead"
   C) "Lightning Rod"
   D) "Mystery Mine"

Extended Trivia!

25. What is Dolly Parton's favorite hobby?

A) Knitting
B) Gardening
C) Painting
D) Fishing

26. What animal is Dolly Parton especially fond of?

A) Cats
B) Birds
C) Dogs
D) Horses

27. Which of Dolly Parton's songs became famous again when Whitney Houston covered it?

A) "Jolene"
B) "9 to 5"
C) "I Will Always Love You"
D) "Coat of Many Colors"

Extended Trivia!

28. How many siblings does Dolly Parton have?

A) 8
B) 9
C) 10
D) 11

29. What year did Dolly Parton open Dollywood?

A) 1982
B) 1986
C) 1990
D) 1994

30. What is Dolly Parton's favorite season?

A) Spring
B) Summer
C) Fall
D) Winter

Extended Trivia!

31. What's the name of Parton's first big hit song?

A) "Jolene"
B) "Coat of Many Colors"
C) "Dumb Blonde"
D) "Here You Come Again"

32. How does Dolly Parton often describe her signature style?

A) Glitzy
B) Classy
C) Simple
D) Rustic

33. What inspired Dolly Parton's song "9 to 5"?

A) Her childhood
B) Her family
C) Her job experiences
D) A movie role

Extended Trivia!

34. What item does Parton always carry with her?

A) A notebook
B) A library card
C) A photo of her mom
D) A lucky charm

35. Which children's album did Dolly Parton create?

A) "Little Dolly"
B) "I Believe in You"
C) "Kid's Country"
D) "Dolly's World"

36. What is the name of Dolly Parton's butterfly garden?

A) Butterfly Haven
B) Butterfly Hill
C) Butterfly Garden
D) Butterfly Retreat

Extended Trivia!

37. Which classic movie is Dolly Parton's favorite?

A) "Gone with the Wind"
B) "The Wizard of Oz"
C) "Casablanca"
D) "It's a Wonderful Life"

38. How many wigs does Dolly Parton have in her collection?

A) 100
B) 200
C) 300
D) 400

39. What hobby does Dolly Parton enjoy that involves a camera?

A) Painting
B) Photography
C) Scrapbooking
D) Filmmaking

Extended Trivia!

40. What special award did Dolly Parton receive from the Country Music Association?

A) Female Vocalist of the Year
B) Album of the Year
C) Entertainer of the Year
D) Song of the Year

41. What kind of garden does Dolly Parton have at her home in Tennessee?

A) Vegetable garden
B) Rose garden
C) Butterfly garden
D) Herb garden

42. What does Dolly Parton love to snack on while watching movies?

A) Chips
B) Popcorn
C) Candy
D) Pretzels

Extended Trivia!

43. Which charitable organization did Dolly Parton create to support literacy?

A) Dolly's Book Club
B) Read with Dolly
C) Imagination Library
D) Dolly's Reading Room

44. What time of day does Dolly Parton prefer to write her songs?

A) Morning
B) Afternoon
C) Evening
D) Night

45. What unique skill does Dolly Parton use when playing guitar?

A) Fingerpicking
B) Acrylic nails as picks
C) Slide guitar
D) Strumming with a coin

Extended Trivia!

46. What is Dolly Parton's favorite holiday?

A) Thanksgiving
B) Halloween
C) Christmas
D) New Year's Eve

47. What did Dolly Parton do with her earnings from her first big hit song?

A) Bought a car
B) Built her parents a house
C) Travelled the world
D) Started a business

48. Who is Dolly Parton's goddaughter?

A) Taylor Swift
B) Miley Cyrus
C) Selena Gomez
D) Demi Lovato

Extended Trivia!

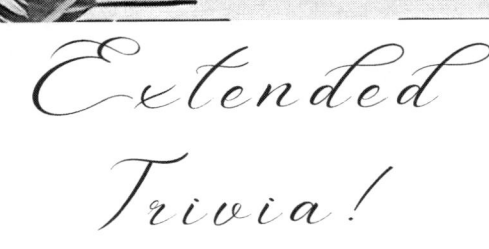

49. What nickname did Dolly Parton give to her wig collection?

A) Wig Wonderland
B) Wig Room
C) Wig Gallery
D) Wig Haven

50. How does Dolly Parton describe her voice?

A) Soft and sweet
B) Loud and proud
C) Unique and special
D) High and clear

51. What classic Christmas song did Dolly Parton cover on her holiday album?

A) "Jingle Bells"
B) "Silent Night"
C) "White Christmas"
D) "Joy to the World"

Answers!

1. A) Dollywood
2. C) "I Will Always Love You"
3. B) 10
4. D) Imagination Library
5. B) Guitar
6. B) "Coat of Many Colors"
7. C) "9 to 5"
8. D) Brunette
9. C) Wigs
10. A) "I Am a Rainbow"
11. B) 13
12. B) Rose
13. A) Backwoods Barbie
14. B) "The Cas Walker Show"
15. B) Camper trailer
16. A) "Jolene"
17. C) 1946
18. B) Tennessee
19. C) "Scent from Above"
20. C) Truvy Jones
21. A) Carl Dean
22. B) Popcorn
23. A) Mick Jagger
24. A) "Wild Eagle"
25. B) Gardening
26. C) Dogs

Answers

27. C) "I Will Always Love You"
28. D) 11
29. B) 1986
30. C) Fall
31. C) "Dumb Blonde"
32. A) Glitzy
33. D) A movie role
34. B) A library card
35. B) "I Believe in You"
36. C) Butterfly garden
37. B) "The Wizard of Oz"
38. C) 300
39. B) Photography
40. C) Entertainer of the Year
41. C) Butterfly garden
42. B) Popcorn
43. C) Imagination Library
44. A) Morning
45. B) Acrylic nails as picks
46. C) Christmas
47. B) Built her parents a house
48. B) Miley Cyrus
49. D) Wig Haven
50. C) Unique and special
51. B) "Silent Night"

Score Card

Person 1: Score _____ / 51

Person 2: Score _____ / 51

Person 3: Score _____ / 51

Person 4: Score _____ / 51

Person 5: Score _____ / 51

Person 6: Score _____ / 51

Person 7: Score _____ / 51

Person 8: Score _____ / 51

Person 9: Score _____ / 51

Person 10: Score _____ / 51

20-26: Dolly Fan

You are on your way to becoming a true Dolly Parton aficionado! As a Dolly Fan, you've shown a keen interest in her life and career. Keep learning and singing along, and you'll soon find yourself knowing all the ins and outs of Dolly's world!

27-33: Rising Dolly Star

Great job! You're exploring the incredible journey of Dolly Parton with enthusiasm and charm. Your knowledge shines bright like Dolly's rhinestones, but there's still more to discover. Keep that passion alive, and you'll be a Dolly expert in no time!

34-40: Dolly Enthusiast

Impressive! You're advancing in your journey through Dolly Parton's amazing life, showcasing a depth of understanding that even her biggest fans would admire. Keep honing your knowledge, and you might just become a Dolly Parton expert!

41-47: Dolly Expert

Congratulations, you're a powerhouse of knowledge when it comes to Dolly Parton! With an understanding as deep as her lyrics, you're navigating through her life and career with the confidence of a true Dolly Expert. Keep this momentum, and you'll be a Dolly legend!

48-51: Dolly Parton Royalty

Spectacular! You've reached a level of expertise that would make even the most dedicated Dolly fans proud. With insight as bright as Dolly's sparkling dresses and a memory as impressive as her song catalog, you're not just a fan – you're the reigning monarch of Dolly Parton trivia!

Dear Reader,

Thank you for joining me on this journey through "101 Facts About Dolly Parton - The Unofficial Kid and Teen Quiz & Trivia Guide to the Country Music Star" Your enthusiasm has made this project truly special.

Creating this book has been a delightful experience, Discovering intriguing details about Dolly and finding inspiration along the way. Each fact represents our desire to honor Dolly's extraordinary life and career.

This book is a labor of love, meant to bring people together in their admiration for Dolly Parton. The stories and moments here are all about passion, joy, and fascination with what makes Dolly so incredible.

Thank you for being part of this journey.

Daisy Jolene

Made in United States
Orlando, FL
26 March 2025